Contents

Introduction to the Yorkshire Dales

An alternative name for the Yorkshire Dales could be the Middle Pennines. To the north, extending through Cumbria, Durham and Northumberland, lies the wild and remote country of the North Pennines, while to the south, eventually merging almost imperceptibly with the Peak District, are the bare gritstone moorlands of the South Pennines. The most distinctive feature of the Yorkshire Dales, which lie between them, is the magnificent limestone landscape which encompasses a major proportion of the area, and around which the National Park is largely based.

Within that area is some of the most attractive countryside in Britain, offering infinite enjoyment and variety to those who are prepared to explore on foot. On the high, exposed moorlands, often buffeted by wind and rain, lonely, austere and dramatic countryside will be encountered. The valleys, however, present a striking contrast: a gentle scene with small woods, riverside meadows and neat green fields separated by miles of drystone walls, dotted with exquisite and unspoilt villages whose welcoming pubs and tea-rooms offer both relaxation and sustenance for the rambler.

It is chiefly the upper and middle reaches of the valleys of the Ribble, Aire, Wharfe, Nidd, Ure and Swale, together with their tributaries and the land between them, that form the Yorkshire Dales. Almost all these rivers flow southwards and eastwards, emerging from their steep-sided valleys into the flatter lands of the vale of York to disgorge their waters first into the Ouse, then the Humber and finally the North Sea. The Ribble is the major exception, turning westwards instead of eastwards, and going through Lancashire and thence into the Irish Sea. Each dale has its own character and individual charms, and it would be impossible even to attempt to draw up a league table of favourites. This would be a pointless task in any case, as all of them are extremely beautiful.

Arranged in an arc around the southern and eastern fringes and serving as gateways into the dales are its main towns — Settle, Skipton, Knaresborough, Ripon and Richmond — mostly built at a point on the river where the narrow dale opens out into broader lowlands. Further up the dales are the smaller towns, some of them little more than villages, such as Grassington, Pateley Bridge, Middleham and Hawes, with Sedbergh standing sentinel at the western approaches to the lesser-known, minor valleys of Dentdale and Garsdale.

Some of the dales are guarded by the grim-looking but impressive remains of medieval castles while, in total contrast, the beauty of certain riverside locations in the lower parts of the dales is enhanced by more mellowed and tranquil monastic ruins. To the east the dales fall away to the flatter, fertile vales of York and Mowbray, to the west they are adjacent to the hills and moorlands of the Bowland and Cumbrian fells, with the smooth and grassy slopes of the Howgills in the north-west acting as a link between the Pennines and the mountains of the Lake District.

The unique landscape of the Yorkshire Dales has been fashioned by the combined forces of both nature and man over an immensely long period of time. Millions of years ago, massive earth movements thrust the Pennines above the surrounding area and also created the series of fractures called the Craven Faults. Here the rocks on one side of the fault have been uplifted high above those on the other side, which have been displaced and buried thousands of feet below. This phenomenon is best observed on Giggleswick Scar, where the line of the fault is followed by the main road from Settle to Kendal. Later, during the Ice Age, huge glaciers flowed along the valleys, deepening and straightening them and smoothing their sides. As they moved, they dropped debris of different rocks at intervals, such as the Norber Erratics overlooking Crummack Dale, a large number of dark gritstone boulders perched conspicuously above the surrounding plateau of white limestone. The scouring effect of the glaciers

Distinctive rock formations at Malham Cove

scraped clean and exposed expanses of bare rock, while torrents of melting water from them were responsible for carving out most of the gorges in the area, such as Gordale Scar near Malham and Trow Gill near Clapham.

Limestone is the predominant rock throughout the Yorkshire Dales and this gives the area its most distinctive scenic features, including many of the most spectacular ones. This is especially true of the Craven area in the south, where the compacted Great Scar limestone (much prized as a building material) comes close to the surface and exhibits all the features of 'karst' scenery, called after the Karst region of Yugoslavia, where similar geological features are to be found. Prominent among these are the great expanses of exposed rock, which gleam white in the sunlight, revealed both in the vertical cliffs or 'scars' and the broad, horizontal terraces or 'pavements'.

It is the action of water, either streams or rainwater, which produces most of the characteristics of limestone scenery. The water absorbs carbon dioxide from the atmosphere to form a weak acid solution, which slowly dissolves the limestone. The action of rainwater can be seen to good effect on

the pavement above Malham Cove, the most visited of all the limestone pavements. Here rainwater has penetrated through cracks in the rock, gradually widening and deepening them to create an almost geometrical pattern of blocks (called 'clints') separated by deep grooves or channels (called 'grikes').

Water will find its way through any joints in the rocks (called sink holes), either seeping through gently or plunging down pot-holes (which are wider and deeper), such as the spectacular Gaping Gill on the lower slopes of Ingleborough, or Hull Pot near the base of Pen-y-ghent. This produces one of the most spectacular features of karst scenery: streams disappearing and flowing underground to leave dry valleys on the surface. As the water penetrates, it continues to dissolve the limestone, eventually creating a network of subterranean caverns, complete with stalactites and stalagmites. Apart from the 'show caves' such as those near Ingleton and Clapham, and the Stump Cross Caverns between Grassington and Pateley Bridge, these are mainly the preserve of pot-holers, and the walker on the surface will only occasionally glimpse their entrances.

Further north, in Wensleydale and

A peaceful scene looking down Swaledale above Muker

Swaledale, the Yoredale series of rocks, called after the ancient name for Wensleydale, are dominant; alternating bands of coarse shales, limestone, sandstone and millstone grit. The differences between weaker and stronger rocks have created the many waterfalls found in this northern part of the dales. Millstone grit is the hardest and most weather-resistant of all these rocks and, where the softer rocks have been worn away, areas of millstone grit remain, standing boldly above the surrounding landscape, either as the major outcrops that cap the summits of the 'Three Peaks' of Ingleborough, Pen-y-ghent and Whernside, or in the form of large groups of individual boulders, like the superb collection at Brimham Rocks overlooking Nidderdale, sculptured into the most incredible and grotesque shapes by the action of wind, rain and frost. In the far north-west, in the Cumbrian section of the dales, much older Silurian slates give rise to a landscape more typical of the highlands, with smooth, steep slopes bisected by deep ravines.

The Yorkshire Dales was never one of the more heavily populated areas of prehistoric Britain, and consequently remains of that period (stone circles and hill forts) are comparatively few and unimpressive, although they do include the highest Iron Age fort in the country, which crowns the summit of Ingleborough, used by the local Brigantes tribe as a defence against the advancing Romans. The Romans likewise left little mark on the area. To them it was a troubled and warlike frontier region and, apart from establishing a few forts linked by roads to secure their control, they largely left it alone. The line of a Roman road running from Ilkley to Bainbridge in Wensleydale, the principal Roman fort in the area, whose grassy ramparts still crown a hill above the village, can be traced for miles across the dales, and parts of it are now put to good purpose as a magnificent scenic footpath (see Walk 9, below).

Most of the settlements were originally founded during the Anglo-Saxon period, either by the Angles who settled in the region following the

departure of the Romans, or by later Viking colonists, both Danish and Norse, from Scandinavia. The Danes penetrated into the area from the east coast, moving up the Humber and Ouse and across the vale of York, while the Norsemen came from the west, by a circuitous route that started in Norway and proceeded via Orkney and Shetland, the Western Isles, Ireland, the Isle of Man and Cumbria. A glance at a map reveals the intermingling of typical Anglo-Saxon place-name endings (-ton, -ham, -den) with the Scandinavian endings (-by, -thorpe, -thwaite), and the predominance of Norse words, such as gill, beck, fell, crag and scar, describing physical features. The word 'dale' itself comes from a Danish word meaning valley.

The Norman barons who accompanied William the Conqueror's successful expedition in 1066 founded churches, created hunting grounds, such as Langstrothdale Chase in Upper Wharfedale, and, most notably, built castles at Skipton, Middleham and Richmond to ensure their rule remained secure. In their wake came the monastic orders, especially the Cistercians, who were attracted to the comparatively remote and sparsely populated Yorkshire Dales because it provided them with the isolation that was an integral part of their code. Abbeys and priories arose on sheltered riverside sites at Bolton in Wharfedale, Jervaulx in Wensleydale, Coverham in Coverdale and Easby in Swaledale. Most imposing of all was Fountains Abbey, the most complete monastic ruin in Britain, which became the wealthiest of all Cistercian monasteries. The monks were great landowners and enterprising managers, clearing forests, improving drainage and developing a thriving sheep-farming industry. Such entrepreneurial skills and financial acumen were to sow the seeds of their future downfall at the hands of Henry VIII in the 1530s.

Scottish raids were a continual threat in the later Middle Ages, which explains why residences continued to be built or rebuilt as fortified strongholds, as happened at Bolton Castle in Wensleydale and Barden Tower, just upstream from Bolton Abbey. Monasteries themselves were sometimes the victims of Scottish raids but, despite this, the development of farming continued. After the monasteries were dissolved, their extensive estates passed into new hands and this, coupled with the removal of the Scottish threat following the union of the crowns in 1603, led to a period of unprecedented prosperity in agriculture, reflected in the extensive rebuilding of farms and manor houses. The two major building booms came during the late seventeenth century and again in the early and middle years of the eighteenth century. Even more than these farms, however, the most widespread and noticeable of all the man-made features in the dales is possibly the hundreds of miles of drystone walling, most of which was erected to separate fields and mark out individual holdings during the height of the enclosure movement in the eighteenth and early nineteenth centuries.

Looking around the area today it may come as a surprise to learn that the Yorkshire Dales has a long history as an industrial as well as a farming area. Lead-mining was carried on for over a thousand years, mainly in Swaledale but also in Nidderdale and Wharfedale, and

Grandstand view of Middle Force at Aysgarth, backed by the church tower

View towards Crummack Dale

only ceased in the early years of the twentieth century. Quarrying, the other major industry has continued to the present day.

Before the construction of roads and the building of the railways, the main form of transportation in the dales was by foot or on horseback, utilising the extensive network of 'green lanes', which are easily recognisable as broad, walled tracks. These are of varying ages and came into being for varying reasons; some may be of prehistoric origin, some were Roman trackways, some were monastic trails linking powerful landowning abbeys like Fountains with their numerous estates, and many were 'drove roads' of later date, along which cattle were driven from their upland pastures in Scotland and northern England to the markets in the Midlands and the south. Nowadays they make excellent walking routes, being generally well surfaced, easy to follow, reasonably straight and fairly free from obstacles. One of the longest and most impressive sections of green lane is Mastiles Lane, which runs for over four miles, linking the former estates of Fountains Abbey around Malham with the monastic grange at Kilnsey in Wharfedale.

Undoubtedly the most spectacular transport undertaking in the dales was the Settle — Carlisle railway, built between 1869 and 1875 as a new alternative route between London and Scotland. It runs across some of the wildest and most inhospitable terrain in the country and its construction was a prodigious feat of Victorian civil engineering. Particularly impressive are the massive stone viaducts, such as Dent Head and Ribblehead, which stride across bleak and windswept countryside. Now, with the inevitable mellowing and acceptance that the passage of time brings, these appear to be almost a part of the landscape, rather than the unwelcome intrusion they seemed initially.

The twentieth century has added at least two new features to the landscape, both of them controversial — conifer plantations and reservoirs, the latter mainly in Upper Nidderdale. But the major impact that the present century has had on the Yorkshire Dales is the growth of mass tourism. The first tourists, apart from a few early intrepid explorers, were the Victorians, who came to view what they thought of as 'picturesque' sights: either natural wonders such as Malham Cove, Hardraw Force and Brimham Rocks, or the man-made, romantic-looking ruins of Bolton Priory and Fountains Abbey. Nowadays tourists flock into the area in ever increasing numbers, chiefly by car, for a wide variety of reasons, many of them of a recreational nature: rock climbing, pot-holing, canoeing, fishing, cycling or, most popular of all, walking.

In 1954 most of the Yorkshire Dales area became one of the ten National Parks of England and Wales. The boundaries were drawn to include, for obvious scenic and geographical reasons, a corner of south-eastern Cumbria, but Nidderdale was excluded, not, it must be emphasised, through any lack of scenic qualities, but because large parts of the upper dale were owned by water authorities and there were a number of reservoirs in the area.

Whether within the National Park boundaries or not, the varied and glorious scenery of the Yorkshire Dales is a paradise for walkers, offering everything from gentle lowland rambles which link attractive riverside villages, to more challenging and longer hikes across the moorland and ascents of some of the well known peaks. The walks in this book embrace all these and illustrate both the scenic variety and the rich historic heritage of this region.

The National Parks and countryside recreation

Ten National Parks were created in England and Wales as a result of an Act of Parliament in 1949. In addition to these, there are numerous specially designated Areas of Outstanding Natural Beauty, Country and Regional Parks, Sites of Special Scientific Interest and picnic areas scattered throughout England, Wales and Scotland, all of which share the twin aims of preservation of the countryside and public accessibility and enjoyment.

In trying to define a National Park, one point to bear in mind is that unlike many overseas ones, Britain's National Parks are not owned by the nation. The vast bulk of the land in them is under private ownership. John Dower, whose report in 1945 created their framework, defined a National Park as 'an extensive area of beautiful and relatively wild country in which, for the nation's benefit and by appropriate national decision and action, (a) the characteristic landscape beauty is strictly preserved, (b) access and facilities for public open-air enjoyment are amply provided, (c) wildlife and buildings and places of architectural and historic interest are suitably protected, while (d) established farming use is effectively maintained'.

The concept of having designated areas of protected countryside grew out of a number of factors that appeared towards the end of the nineteenth century; principally greater facilities and opportunities for travel, the development of various conservationist bodies and the establishment of National Parks abroad. Apart from a few of the early individual travellers such as Celia Fiennes and Daniel Defoe, who were usually more concerned with commenting on agricultural improvements, the appearance of towns and the extent of antiquities to be found than with the wonders of nature, interest in the countryside as a source of beauty, spiritual refreshment and recreation, and, along with that, an interest in

conserving it, did not arise until the Victorian era. Towards the end of the eighteenth century, improvements in road transport enabled the wealthy to visit regions that had hitherto been largely inaccessible and, by the middle of the nineteenth century, the construction of the railways opened up such possibilities to the middle classes and, later on, to the working classes in even greater numbers. At the same time, the Romantic movement was in full swing and, encouraged by the works of Wordsworth, Coleridge and Shelley, interest and enthusiasm for wild places, including the mountain, moorland and hill regions of northern and western Britain, were now in vogue. Eighteenth-century taste had thought of the Scottish Highlands, the Lake District and Snowdonia as places to avoid, preferring controlled order and symmetry in nature as well as in architecture and town planning. But upper and middle class Victorian travellers were thrilled and awed by what they saw as the untamed savagery and wilderness of mountain peaks, deep and secluded gorges, thundering waterfalls, towering cliffs and rocky crags. In addition, there was a growing reaction against the materialism and squalor of Victorian industrialisation and urbanisation and a desire to escape from the formality and artificiality of town life into areas of unspoilt natural beauty.

A result of this was the formation of a number of different societies, all concerned with the 'great outdoors': naturalist groups, rambling clubs and conservationist organisations. One of the earliest of these was the Commons, Open Spaces and Footpaths Preservation Society, originally founded in 1865 to preserve commons and develop public access to the countryside. Particularly influential was the National Trust, set up in 1895 to protect and maintain both places of natural beauty and places of historic interest, and, later on, the Councils for the Preservation of Rural England, Wales and Scotland, three separate bodies that came into being between 1926 and 1928.

The world's first National Park was the Yellowstone Park in the United States, designated in 1872. This was followed by others in Canada, South Africa, Germany, Switzerland, New

Zealand and elsewhere, but in Britain such places did not come about until after the Second World War. Proposals for the creation of areas of protected countryside were made before the First World War and during the 1920s and 1930s, but nothing was done. The growing demand from people in towns for access to open country and the reluctance of landowners – particularly those who owned large expanses of uncultivated moorland – to grant it led to a number of ugly incidents, in particular the mass trespass in the Peak District in 1932, when fighting took place between ramblers and game-keepers and some of the trespassers received stiff prison sentences.

It was in the climate exemplified by the Beveridge Report and the subsequent creation of the welfare state, however, that calls for country-side conservation and access came to fruition in parliament. Based on the recommendations of the Dower Report (1945) and the Hobhouse Committee (1947), the National Parks and Country-side Act of 1949 provided for the designation and preservation of areas both of great scenic beauty and of particular wildlife and scientific interest throughout Britain. More specifically it provided for the creation of National Parks in England and Wales. Scotland was excluded because, with greater areas of open space and a smaller population, there were fewer pressures on the Scottish countryside and there-fore there was felt to be less need for the creation of such protected areas.

A National Parks Commission was set up, and over the next eight years ten areas were designated as parks; seven in England (Northumberland, Lake District, North York Moors, Yorkshire Dales, Peak District, Exmoor and Dartmoor) and three in Wales (Snowdonia, Brecon Beacons and Pembrokeshire Coast). At the same time the Commission was also given the responsibility for designating other smaller areas of high recreational and scenic qualities (Areas of Outstanding Natural Beauty), plus the power to propose and develop long-distance footpaths, now called National Trails,

though it was not until 1965 that the first of these, the Pennine Way, came into existence.

Further changes came with the Countryside Act of 1968 (a similar one for Scotland had been passed in 1967). The National Parks Commission was replaced by the Countryside Commission, which was now to oversee and review virtually all aspects of country-side conservation, access and provision of recreational amenities. The Country Parks, which were smaller areas of countryside often close to urban areas, came into being. A number of long-distance footpaths were created, followed by an even greater number of unofficial long- or middle-distance paths, devised by individuals, ramblers' groups or local authorities. Provision of car parks and visitor centres, way-marking of public rights of way and the production of leaflets giving suggestions for walking routes all increased, a reflection both of increased leisure and of a greater desire for recreational activity, of which walking in particular, now recognised as the most popular leisure pursuit, has had a great explosion of interest.

The authorities who administer the individual National Parks have the very difficult task of reconciling the interests of the people who live and earn their living within them with those of the visitors. National Parks, and the other designated areas, are not living museums. Developments of various kinds, in housing, transport and rural industries, are needed. There is pressure to exploit the resources of the area, through more intensive farming, or through increased quarrying and forestry, extraction of minerals or the construction of reservoirs.

In the end it all comes down to a question of balance; a balance between conservation and 'sensitive develop-ment'. On the one hand there is a responsibility to preserve and enhance the natural beauty of the National Parks and to promote their enjoyment by the public, and on the other, the needs and well-being of the people living and working in them have to be borne in mind.

The National Trust

Anyone who likes visiting places of natural beauty and/or historic interest has cause to be grateful to the National Trust. Without it, many such places would probably have vanished by now, either under an avalanche of concrete and bricks and mortar or through reservoir construction or blanket afforestation.

It was in response to the pressures on the countryside posed by the relentless march of Victorian industrialisation that the Trust was set up in 1895. Its founders, inspired by the common goals of protecting and conserving Britain's national heritage and widening public access to it, were Sir Robert Hunter, Octavia Hill and Canon Rawnsley; a solicitor, a social reformer and a clergyman respectively. The latter was particularly influential. As a canon of Carlisle Cathedral and vicar of Crosthwaite (near Keswick), he was concerned about threats to the Lake District and had already been active in protecting footpaths and promoting public access to open countryside. After the flooding of Thirlmere in 1879 to create a large reservoir, he and his two colleagues became increasingly convinced that the only effective protection was outright ownership of land.

The purpose of the National Trust is to preserve areas of natural beauty and sites of historic interest by acquisition, holding them in trust for the nation and making them available for public access and enjoyment. Some of its properties have been acquired through purchase, but many have been donated. Nowadays it is one of the biggest landowners in the country and protects over half a million acres of land, including nearly 500 miles of coastline and a large number of historic properties (mostly houses) in England, Wales and Northern Ireland. (There is a separate National Trust for Scotland, which was set up in 1931.)

Furthermore, once a piece of land has come under Trust ownership, it is difficult for its status to be altered. As a result of Parliamentary legislation in 1907, the Trust was given the right to declare its property inalienable, so ensuring that in any dispute it can appeal directly to Parliament.

As it works towards its dual aims of conserving areas of attractive countryside and encouraging greater public access (not easy to reconcile in this age of mass tourism), the Trust provides an excellent service to walkers by creating new concessionary paths and waymarked trails, by maintaining stiles and footbridges and by combating the ever increasing problem of footpath erosion.

The Ramblers' Association

No organisation works more actively to protect and extend the rights and interests of walkers in the countryside than the Ramblers' Association. Its aims (summarised here) are clear: to foster a greater knowledge, love and care of the countryside; to assist in the protection and enhancement of public rights of way and areas of natural beauty; to work for greater public access to the countryside and to encourage more people to take up rambling as a healthy, recreational activity.

It was founded in 1935 when, following the setting up of a National Council of Ramblers' Federation in 1931, a number of federations earlier formed in London, Manchester, the Midlands and elsewhere came together to create a more effective pressure group, to deal with such contemporary problems as the disappearance and obstruction of footpaths, the prevention of access to open mountain and moorland and increasing hostility from landowners. This was the era of the mass trespasses, when there were sometimes violent confrontations between ramblers and gamekeepers, especially on the moorlands of the Peak District.

Since then the Ramblers' Association has played an influential role in preserving and developing the national footpath network, supporting the creation of National Parks and encouraging the designation and way-marking of long-distance footpaths.

Our freedom to walk in the countryside is precarious, and requires constant vigilance. As well as the perennial problems of footpaths being illegally obstructed, disappearing through lack of use or extinguished by housing or road construction, new dangers can spring up at any time.

It is to meet such problems and dangers that the Ramblers' Association exists and represents the interests of all walkers. The address to write to for information on the Ramblers' Association and how to become a member is given on page 78.

Walkers and the law

The average walker in a National Park or other popular walking area, armed with the appropriate Ordnance Survey map, reinforced perhaps by a guidebook giving detailed walking instructions, is unlikely to run into legal difficulties, but it is useful to know something about the law relating to public rights of way. The right to walk over certain parts of the countryside has developed over a long period of time, and how such rights came into being and how far they are protected by the law is a complex subject, fascinating in its own right, but too lengthy to be discussed here. The following comments are intended simply to be a helpful guide, backed up by the Countryside Access Charter, a concise summary of walkers' rights and obligations drawn up by the Countryside Commission.

Basically there are two main kinds of public rights of way: footpaths (for walkers only) and bridle-ways (for walkers, riders on horseback and pedal cyclists). Footpaths and bridle-ways are shown by broken green lines on Ordnance Survey Pathfinder and Outdoor Leisure maps and broken red lines on Landranger maps. There is also a third category, called byways or 'roads used as a public path': chiefly broad, walled tracks (green lanes) or farm roads, which walkers, riders and cyclists have to share, usually only occasionally, with motor vehicles. Many of these public paths have been in existence for hundreds of years and some even originated as prehistoric trackways and have been in constant use for well over 2,000 years.

The term 'right of way' means exactly what it says. It gives right of passage over what, in the vast majority of cases, is private land, and you are required to keep to the line of the path and not stray onto the land either side. If you inadvertently wander off the right of way — either because of faulty map-reading or because the route is not clearly indicated on the ground — you are technically trespassing and the wisest course is to ask the nearest available person (farmer or fellow walker) to direct you back to the correct route. There are stories of unpleasant confrontations between walkers and farmers at times, but in general most farmers are helpful and co-operative when responding to a genuine and polite request for assistance in route finding.

Obstructions can sometimes be a problem and probably the commonest of these is where a path across a field has been ploughed up. It is legal for a farmer to plough up a path provided that he restores it within two weeks, barring exceptionally bad weather. This does not always happen and here the walker is presented with a dilemma. Does he follow the line of the path, even if this inevitably means treading on crops, or does he use his common sense and walk around the edge of the field? The latter course of action often seems the best but, as this means that you would be trespassing, you are, in law, supposed to keep to the exact line of the path, avoiding unnecessary damage to crops. In the case of other obstructions which may block a path (illegal fences and locked gates etc.), common sense again has to be used in order to negotiate them by the easiest method (detour or removal), followed by reporting the matter to the local council or National Park authority.

Apart from rights of way enshrined by law, there are a number of other paths available to walkers. Permissive or concessionary paths have been created where a landowner has given permission for the public to use a particular route across his land. The main problem with these is that, as they have been granted as a concession, there is no legal right to use them and therefore they can be extinguished at any time. In practice, many of these concessionary routes have been established on land owned either by large public bodies such as the Forestry Commission or the water authorities, or by a private one, such as the National Trust, and as these mainly encourage walkers to use their paths, they are unlikely to be closed unless a change of ownership occurs.

Walkers also have free access to Country Parks (except where requested to keep away from certain areas for ecological reasons e.g. wildlife protection, woodland regeneration, safeguarding of rare plants etc.), canal towpaths and most beaches. By custom, though not by right, you are generally free to walk across the open and uncultivated higher land of mountain, moorland and fell, but this varies from area to area and from one season to another — grouse moors, for example, will be out of bounds during the breeding and shooting seasons and some open areas are used as Ministry of Defence firing ranges, for which reason access will be restricted. In some areas the situation has been clarified as a result of 'access agreements' between the landowners and either the county council or the National Park authority, which clearly define when and where you can walk over such open country.

Countryside Access Charter

Your rights of way are:

- Public footpaths — on foot only. Sometimes waymarked in yellow
- Bridle-ways — on foot, horseback and pedal cycle. Sometimes waymarked in blue
- Byways (usually old roads), most 'roads used as public paths' and, of course, public roads — all traffic has the right of way.

Use maps, signs and waymarks to check rights of way. Ordnance Survey Pathfinder and Landranger maps show most public rights of way

On rights of way you can:

- take a pram, pushchair or wheelchair if practicable
- take a dog (on a lead or under close control)
- take a short route round an illegal obstruction or remove it sufficiently to get past

You have a right to go for recreation to:

- public parks and open spaces — on foot
- most commons near older towns and cities — on foot and sometimes on horseback
- private land where the owner has a formal agreement with the local authority

In addition you can use the following by local or established custom or consent, but ask for advice if you are unsure:

- many areas of open country, such as moorland, fell and coastal areas, especially those in the care of the National Trust, and some commons
- some woods and forests, especially those owned by the Forestry Commission
- Country Parks and picnic sites
- most beaches
- canal towpaths
- some private paths and tracks

Consent sometimes extends to horse-riding and cycling

For your information:

- county councils and London boroughs maintain and record rights of way, and register commons
- obstructions, dangerous animals, harassment and misleading signs on rights of way are illegal and you should report them to the county council
- paths across fields can be ploughed, but must normally be reinstated within two weeks
- landowners can require you to leave land to which you have no right of access
- motor vehicles are normally permitted only on roads, byways and some 'roads used as public paths'

Ingleborough — a brooding but familiar giant

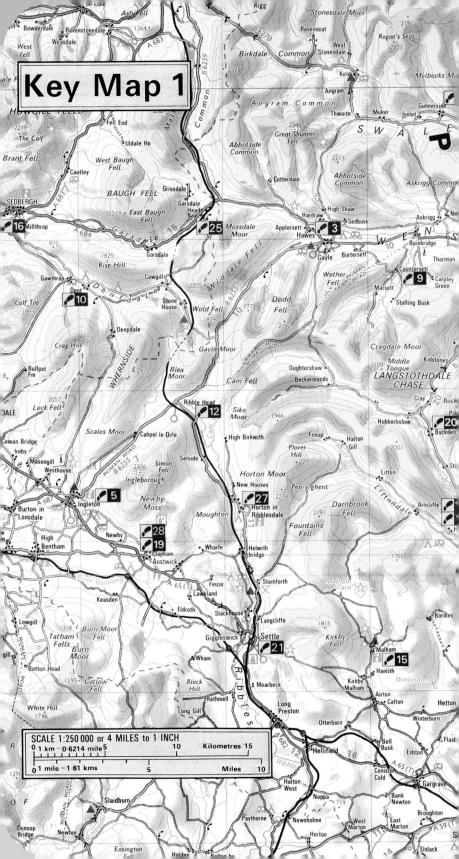

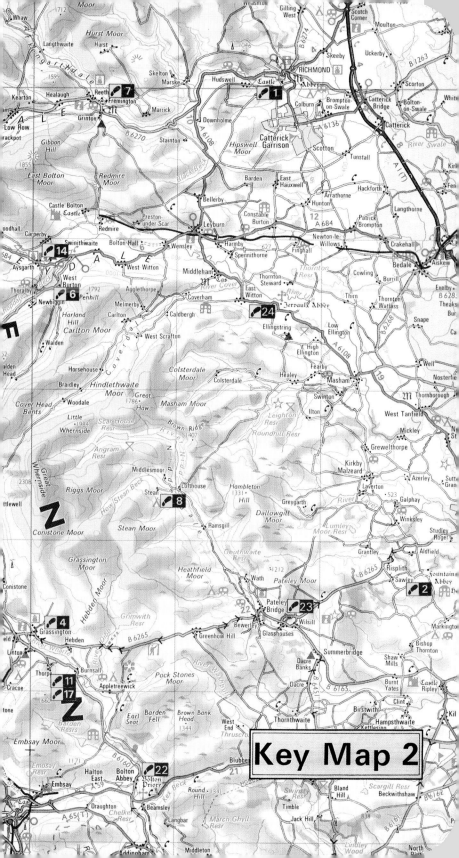

Key Map 2

CONVENTIONAL SIGNS 1:25 000 or $2\frac{1}{2}$ INCHES to 1 MILE

ROADS AND PATHS

Not necessarily rights of way

M I or A 6(M) | M I or A 6(M) — Motorway

A 31 (T) | A 31(T) — Trunk road

A 35 | A 35 — Main road

B 3074 | B 3074 — Secondary road

(Trunk road, Main road, Secondary road: Narrow roads with passing places are annotated)

A 35 | A 35 — Dual carriageway

Road generally more than 4m wide

Road generally less than 4m wide

Other road, drive or track

Unfenced roads and tracks are shown by pecked lines

Path

RAILWAYS

Multiple track } Standard gauge

Single track } Standard gauge

Narrow gauge

Siding

Cutting

Embankment

Tunnel

Road over & under

Level crossing; station

PUBLIC RIGHTS OF WAY

Public rights of way may not be evident on the ground

Public paths { Footpath, Bridleway

Byway open to all traffic

Road used as a public path

DANGER AREA

MOD ranges in the area
Danger!
Observe warning notices

The indication of a towpath in this book does not necessarily imply a public right of way

The representation of any other road, track or path is no evidence of the existence of a right of way

BOUNDARIES

County (England and Wales)

District

London Borough

Civil Parish (England)* Community (Wales)

Constituency (County, Borough, Burgh or European Assembly)

Coincident boundaries are shown by the first appropriate symbol

*For Ordnance Survey purposes County Boundary is deemed to be the limit of the parish structure whether or not a parish area adjoins

SYMBOLS

Church or chapel { with tower, with spire, without tower or spire

Glasshouse; youth hostel

Bus or coach station

Lighthouse; lightship; beacon

Triangulation station

Triangulation point on { church or chapel, lighthouse, beacon, building; chimney

pylon pole — Electricity transmission line

VILLA — Roman antiquity (AD 43 to AD 420)

Castle — Other antiquities

Site of antiquity

1066 — Site of battle (with date)

Gravel pit

Sand pit

Chalk pit, clay pit or quarry

Refuse or slag heap

Sloping wall

Water

Mud

Sand; sand & shingle

National Park or Forest Park Boundary

NT — National Trust always open

NT — National Trust opening restricted

FC — Forestry Commission

VEGETATION

Limits of vegetation are defined by positioning of the symbols but may be delineated also by pecks or dots

Coniferous trees

Non-coniferous trees

Coppice

Orchard

Scrub

Bracken, rough grassland

In some areas bracken ( ) and rough grassland ( ) are shown separately

Heath

(Bracken, rough grassland; Heath: Shown collectively as rough grassland on some sheets)

Reeds

Marsh

Saltings

HEIGHTS AND ROCK FEATURES

50 / 285 — Determined by { ground survey, air survey

Surface heights are to the nearest metre above mean sea level. Heights shown close to a triangulation pillar refer to the station height at ground level and not necessarily to the summit

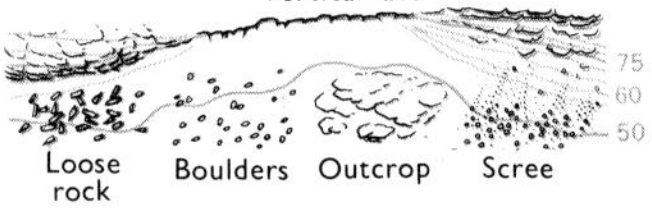

Vertical face
75
60
50
Loose rock
Boulders
Outcrop
Scree

Contours are at 5 metres vertical interval

ABBREVIATIONS 1:25 000 or $2\frac{1}{2}$ INCHES to 1 MILE also 1:10 000/1:10 560 or 6 INCHES to 1 MILE

BP,BS	Boundary Post or Stone
CH	Club House
F V	Ferry Foot or Vehicle
FB	Foot Bridge
HO	House
MP,MS	Mile Post or Stone
Mon	Monument
P	Post Office
Pol Sta	Police Station
PC	Public Convenience
PH	Public House
Sch	School
Spr	Spring
T	Telephone, public
A,R	Telephone, AA or RAC
TH	Town Hall
Twr	Tower
W	Well
Wd Pp	Wind Pump

Abbreviations applicable only to 1:10 000/1:10 560 or 6 INCHES to 1 MILE

Ch	Church
F Sta	Fire Station
Fn	Fountain
GP	Guide Post
P	Pole or Post
S	Stone
TCB	Telephone Call Box
TCP	Telephone Call Post
Y	Youth Hostel

TOURIST INFORMATION

✝ Abbey, Cathedral, Priory

🐟 Aquarium

△ Camp site

🚐 Caravan site

🏰 Castle

🕳 Cave

🏚 Country park

⚲ Craft centre

🅿 Parking

°C Public Convenience (in rural areas)

Ⅱ Ancient Monuments and Historic Buildings
in the care of the Secretary

◆ Long Distance or Recreational Path

ennine Way Named path

❁ Garden

⚑ Golf course or links

🏛 Historic house

ℹ Information centre

🏍 Motor racing

🖼 Museum

❗ Nature or forest trail

🦆 Nature reserve

𝕮𝖆𝖘𝖙𝖑𝖊
SAILING Selected places of interest

📞 T Public telephone

⊕ Mountain rescue post

NATIONAL PARK Boundary of National Park access land
ACCESS LAND Private land for which the National Park Planning Board
have negotiated public access

◄ Access Point

☆ Other tourist feature

✕ Picnic site

🚂 Preserved railway

🏇 Racecourse

⛷ Skiing

☀ Viewpoint

🦌 Wildlife park

🐘 Zoo

WALKS

1 Start point of walk

➤ Route of walk

▬ Featured walk

FOLLOW THE COUNTRY CODE

Enjoy the countryside and respect its life and work

Guard against all risk of fire

Fasten all gates

Keep your dogs under close control

Keep to public paths across farmland

Leave livestock, crops and machinery alone

Use gates and stiles to cross fences, hedges and walls

Take your litter home

Help to keep all water clean

Protect wildlife, plants and trees

Take special care on country roads

Make no unnecessary noise

1 Richmond and Easby

Start:	Richmond
Distance:	3½ miles (5·5 km)
Approximate time:	1½ hours
Parking:	Richmond
Refreshments:	Plenty of pubs, restaurants and cafés in Richmond
Ordnance Survey maps:	Landranger 92 (Barnard Castle) and 99 (Northallerton & Ripon), First Series NZ 10 (Richmond) and SE 19 (Catterick Camp)

General description *A relaxing, easy, half-day stroll which leaves plenty of time to explore the fascinating and picturesque town of Richmond. It is ideal for children, with good paths across riverside meadows and woods, some splendid views up and down the Swale and two attractive and interesting ruins, one military and the other ecclesiastical, to excite the imagination.*

It is a most pleasant experience to wander around the streets of Richmond, one of the great historic towns of England. This is a supremely attractive and photogenic old market town, set on a hilltop above a particularly beautiful wooded stretch of the Swale, with portions of its medieval walls and gateways remaining, narrow winding streets coupled with broad and elegant Georgian thoroughfares, a spacious sloping Market Place, two medieval churches and the tower of a Franciscan friary. Inevitably the great Norman castle, which occupies a

triangular area on a cliff above the river guarding the entrance to Swaledale, dominates the town. It was founded by Alan the Red of Brittany just after the Norman Conquest and still retains a part of the original eleventh-century castle, known as Scolland's Hall, one of the earliest domestic buildings in the country. The rest of the castle, including the curtain walls and tall keep, date from the twelfth century. Despite its size and apparent impregnability, Richmond Castle enjoyed an uneventful existence and its walls were never put to the test.

The walk begins at the top end of the huge Market Place. Start by walking past All Saints Church down to the bottom end of the market and turning right along Millgate, which winds down to the river. By a small car park **(A)** turn left along the riverside path and, keeping close to the river all the time, walk across a picnic area and under a bridge. Shortly afterwards, turn sharp left away from the river and, about 50 yards (46 m) ahead, turn right along a broad track. Follow this track through the attractive woods that clothe the steep cliffs above the Swale, pausing now and then to look back and admire the fine views of Richmond. Soon the path drops down to regain the river-bank and keeps along it for just under ½ mile (0·8 km). On approaching Easby go up some steps, climb a stile and continue to the abbey ruins a little way ahead.

Easby Abbey occupies an enviably tranquil position on the banks of the Swale and, apart from occasional Scottish raids, always seems to have led a peaceful history. It was a house of Premonstratensian canons, founded in 1155 and dissolved in 1536. The church is the least substantial surviving portion, and little

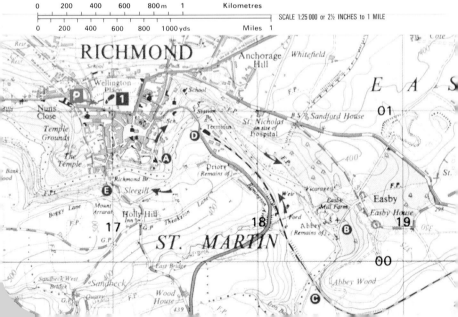

Richmond — town and castle above the River Swale

apart from the presbytery is left, but there are extensive remains of the domestic buildings, notably the infirmary, dormitory and refectory. Next to the ruins stands the small thirteenth-century parish church. Because the inhabitants of the abbey were canons rather than monks, they could act as the local parish priests, which they did until the Dissolution.

Before continuing along the riverside path, it is worthwhile making a short detour up the lane in order to take in a comprehensive view of both the historic buildings in one glance. Below is Easby Abbey, lying amidst riverside meadows, with Richmond Castle dominating the skyline on the horizon.

Keep along the riverside path **(B)**, through more woodland and, where the paths fork, bear slightly left along the higher one. Turn right over a disused railway bridge **(C)** to cross the Swale, and continue along the track of the former railway for about a mile (1·5 km) to Station Bridge on the edge of

Richmond. Gaps in the hedges that line both sides reveal more fine views, initially of the abbey over to the right and, in the later stages, of the buildings of Richmond, clustered high above the river.

Pass through the site of the former station, now used as a picnic and recreation area and, just before reaching the road, turn right down steps to the river-bank and then left **(D)**, under Station Bridge and over a stile, along a riverside path. Bearing slightly left uphill, climb a stile, keep ahead to another stile, climb that and continue downhill through trees back to the river, opposite a most dramatic view of the castle towering above its rocky cliff. Turn right over the next bridge **(E)**, Richmond Bridge, into the town and keep ahead for a few yards before turning right again and ascending Cornforth Hill. Continue through a gate in one of the few surviving sections of Richmond's medieval walls, and along the Bar back to the top end of the Market Place.

2 Fountains Abbey

Start:	Fountains Abbey
Distance:	4½ miles (7·25 km)
Approximate time:	2½ hours
Parking:	Fountains Abbey
Refreshments:	Café at Fountains Abbey
Ordnance Survey maps:	Landranger 99 (Northallerton & Ripon), Pathfinder SE 26/36 653 (Fountains Abbey and Boroughbridge) and SE 27/37 641 (Ripon)

General description *Much of this walk falls within the boundaries of Studley Royal Country Park, which is owned and maintained by the National Trust and includes Fountains Abbey. The abbey, the most complete and extensive monastic remains in Europe, is the centre-piece of the park, but is by no means the only attraction. Within a fairly short circuit there is an unusually varied mixture of interesting things to see: farmland and deer park, eighteenth-century water gardens and a nineteenth-century church, the seventeenth-century hall, and, of course, the medieval abbey itself, which makes a spectacular climax. The terrain is gentle throughout, making for a walk which is at the same time both relaxing and thoroughly fascinating.*

The abbey comes at the end of the walk. Start by turning right out of the car park, along the road to Harrogate, following it as it curves uphill by the side of the boundary wall

Fountains Abbey in its parkland setting

of the abbey. Just past a stream turn left over a stile **(A)**, at a public footpath sign, along a clearly defined and well waymarked path. From this path there is soon a spectacular and comprehensive view of the extensive remains of the abbey, and Fountains Hall, down in the valley on the left, an early appetiser for treats in store.

Pass through two gates, keep round the right-hand side of a farm and continue along the edge of a field, by a hedge on the right. Where that hedge ends, bear left downhill to a gate near the edge of a wood, go through it and take the path through the wood. One of the ruined entrances to the Studley Royal estate is soon passed on the left and in front there are fine views over Ripon, with its cathedral towers standing prominently, and the Vale of York, backed by the long line of the Hambleton Hills, western edge of the North York Moors.

Descend to a crossroads of tracks and turn sharp left **(B)** to continue down through a steep-sided, wooded valley. At the bottom, cross a footbridge over the River Skell near a ford, turn right and follow a broad track uphill, leaving the woods at the top of the ridge and emerging into open country. Approaching the village of Studley Roger, the rough track becomes a tarmac drive and, just before the village, turn left **(C)** to enter Studley Royal Country Park.

The deer park was created in the sixteenth century, but its present appearance dates mainly from 1699, when the estate came into the ownership of John Aislabie. He was an ambitious and wealthy landowner who, for a time, was Chancellor of the Exchequer before being forced to resign, even serving a brief spell of imprisonment, through his involvement in the South Sea Bubble, a financial scandal which came to light in 1720. After this enforced retirement from public life, he concentrated on his estates here in Yorkshire, in particular, transforming part of them into a landscaped water garden. His great ambition was to acquire the ruins of Fountains Abbey and make them the main attraction of his grand design – the ultimate garden ornament – but this dream was realised by his son, William, who purchased the neighbouring estate, which included Fountains Abbey and the hall, after his father's death.

Walk along the drive, through the elegant eighteenth-century gateway, into the deer park. Now pause and look back. The towers of Ripon Cathedral are aligned exactly with the drive – part of John Aislabie's scheme to have Ripon Cathedral at one end and Fountains Abbey at the other end of his park. Continue ahead to a junction of park roads. The route turns left to the lakeside **(D)** but it is worthwhile keeping ahead for a few

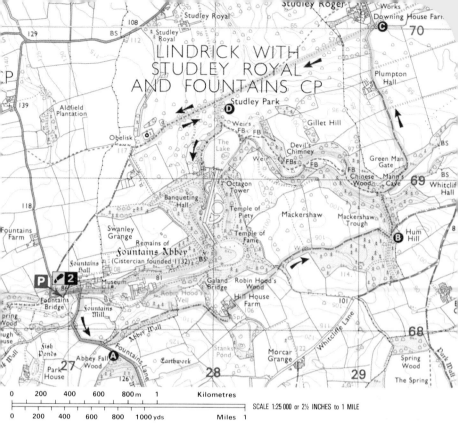

SCALE 1:25 000 or 2½ INCHES to 1 MILE

hundred yards to take a look at the ornate Victorian church, the spire of which has been visible for quite a while, built for the Marquis of Ripon by William Burges in the 1870s at the opposite end to Ripon Cathedral of the grand avenue formed by the drive.

After turning left to the lakeside, continue to the restaurant near where you pay to enter the landscaped gardens and abbey ruins. Now comes a most enjoyable stroll of just under a mile (1·5 km) through the gardens, keeping to the main path as it threads its way round small lakes, canals and cascades, past classical temples, across lawns and through woods, all carefully planned and linked together to create pleasing vistas. Finally keep along the river-bank for the finest view of all – the first stunning sight of the abbey ruins themselves, the climax of the walk, as John Aislabie intended.

Fountains Abbey was founded in 1132 by a group of Benedictine monks from St Mary's Abbey in York who were discontented with the lax standards there. They were granted land in what was then the remote wilderness of Skelldale by the Archbishop of York and, over the next two centuries, built up what was to be the wealthiest Cistercian monastery in England. At the height of its powers, in the thirteenth and fourteenth centuries, it owned vast areas of land in the Yorkshire Dales: arable land, sheep pastures, fisheries,

lead-mines and quarries. Like other large monasteries, it was dissolved in 1539 by Henry VIII but its comparative remoteness from towns and villages has ensured that its buildings have remained almost intact, save for roofs and windows. As a consequence it reveals the buildings, layout and way of life of a great medieval monastery more fully than any other site in the country.

The church, built in the late twelfth century, is 300 ft (91 m) long. Particularly impressive is the nave, an outstanding example of Transitional architecture, the thirteenth-century Chapel of the Nine Altars at the east end, and the 170 ft-(52 m-)high tower, built in the fifteenth century above the north transept instead of, as would usually be the case, above the centre of the church. The domestic buildings grouped round the cloisters (chapter house, refectories, dormitories, kitchens, cellars, guest houses and the private residence of the abbot) are, unusually, intact and clearly indicate that this was not just a religious establishment, but the heart of a vast business empire.

From the abbey continue along a drive, passing on the right the fine mansion of Fountains Hall, built in the early seventeenth century by Sir Richard Gresham, one of the inheritors of the monastic estates, partly using stones from the abbey. The drive leads to the road and car park.

21

3 Hawes and Hardraw Force

Start:	Hawes
Distance:	4½ miles (7·25 km)
Approximate time:	2½ hours
Parking:	National Park car park at Hawes
Refreshments:	Pubs and cafés in Hawes, pub and café at Hardraw
Ordnance Survey maps:	Landranger 98 (Wensleydale & Upper Wharfedale) and Outdoor Leisure 30 (Yorkshire Dales – Northern & Central areas)

General description *This round trip from Hawes, a pleasant and relaxing half-day stroll, provides extensive views over Wensleydale and includes a visit to Hardraw Force. Here a great sheet of water drops 96 ft (29 m), making it the highest single fall in the Dales.*

Hawes, the main centre of Upper Wensleydale, is a popular and bustling market town hemmed in to both north and south by high fells. Solid, stone buildings, dating from the seventeenth to the nineteenth centuries, line its market place and narrow streets, and Gayle Beck makes a fine sight as it tumbles through the town centre, under Hawes Bridge, on its way to join the River Ure. One of Hawes' other claims to fame is that it is the home of Wensleydale cheese.

Start at the National Park car park and information centre, on the site of the former railway station, and turn right along the road signposted to Hardraw and Muker, soon turning left through a gate, at a Pennine Way sign, along a straight, paved path. Rejoin the road and follow it over the Ure. Ignoring a footpath sign to Hardraw, continue along the road for another 100 yards (92 m) and, just after it begins to climb, turn left **(A)** up some steps, through a gate, at a Pennine Way sign, and along the clear path ahead. In front is a fine view of Great Shunner Fell, which is 2,340 ft (716 m) high. For much of the way the path is paved and you keep along it over several stiles to Hardraw, coming out into the village **(B)** opposite the church and Green Dragon Inn.

Hardraw Force is on private land behind the Green Dragon and, in order to see it, you have to go into the inn (staying a while if you like), pay a small fee, pass straight through, out of the back door and along a path by the church on the left. Entering a narrow, wooded gorge, the majestic drop is suddenly seen ahead. It is possible to walk behind the fall but this is inadvisable; the passage of so many feet have made the rocks smooth, slippery and potentially dangerous.

Retrace your steps back through the inn to the village, turn left and left again at the side of the inn. Go through a gap, up some steps, keep ahead by a wall on the left, climb a stile and follow an uphill path. Continue up more

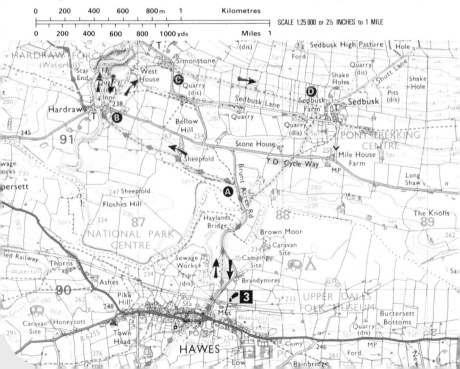

SCALE 1:25 000 or 2½ INCHES to 1 MILE

The impressive drop of Hardraw Force

steps, over another stile and carry on uphill, passing a house on the right. At the corner of this house, go through a gate and keep straight ahead to another gate by a barn. Pass through that and continue, by a wall on the left, to the drive of the Simonstone Hall Hotel. Turn right down the drive to a road (C), climb a stone stile on the opposite side, at a public footpath sign to Sedbusk, and keep ahead, joining a broad farm track on the left. Near farm buildings, climb two ladder stiles and continue ahead in a straight line across a series of small fields and through a succession of gates and stiles, heading towards the houses of the village in front.

In the penultimate field before the houses, turn sharp right (D), along a reasonably distinct path, to a stone stile at the end of that field. Climb it, turn right along the road for a few yards, and then turn left over a stile, at a public footpath sign for Haylands Bridge. Take the downhill path ahead, bear slightly right to a ladder stile, climb over and keep ahead to a stone stile. Climb that and, with the buildings of Hawes and the bridge over the Ure clearly visible in front, continue over the brow of the hill down to a road. Go straight across, through a gate opposite and continue across the next field towards the bridge. Climb a stile, head down to a footbridge and continue to the road. Here turn left and retrace the first part of the outward route back to Hawes.

4 Grassington and the River Wharfe

Start:	Grassington
Distance:	4½ miles (7·25 km)
Approximate time:	2½ hours
Parking:	National Park car park in Grassington
Refreshments:	Pubs and cafés in Grassington
Ordnance Survey maps:	Landranger 98 (Wensleydale & Upper Wharfedale) and Outdoor Leisure 10 (Yorkshire Dales – Southern area)

General description *Grassington, capital of Upper Wharfedale, is a rambler's paradise, with moorland, woodland and riverside paths radiating from it in all directions. This easy and pleasant walk takes in some of the finest features of its immediate locality – roughly one third is across open moorland, one third through delightful woodland and the final third along one of the most attractive stretches of the Wharfe.*

From the car park turn left and shortly afterwards right, up to Grassington's bustling cobbled market square, lined with plenty of shops, inns and cafés. Most of the fine old stone houses and cottages date from the seventeenth to the nineteenth centuries, when the small farming village expanded as it became the centre of local lead-mining, textile and quarrying industries. Apart from quarrying, all these have now gone and Grassington's present prosperity is firmly based on tourism.

Continue up the main street and, at the top **(A)**, turn left along Chapel Street, past houses and cottages, to Town Head. Here is a particularly fine seventeenth-century yeoman farmer's house. Keep ahead through a farmyard at a public footpath sign to Conistone, bear left between barns at another footpath sign and, at a path junction, keep ahead along the right-hand fork. Follow the path over several stone stiles, entering Lea Green after the last stile, the site of ancient settlements and containing a number of the limestone pavements that are such a striking feature of much of the scenery of the Yorkshire Dales. All around are fine views, especially to the left over Wharfedale and Grass Wood.

Keep bearing left towards the wall that borders the wood and, approaching a gorge in front, look out for a ladder stile on the left **(B)**. Climb over and keep ahead along a grassy path between two small hills to enter Bastow Wood. At a junction of paths, bear slightly right and continue ahead through this most distinctive area of limestone knolls, open glades and widely-spaced trees. At a

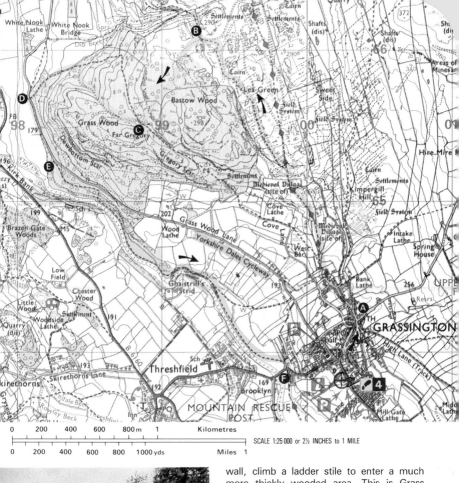

wall, climb a ladder stile to enter a much more thickly wooded area. This is Grass Wood, a nature reserve owned and maintained by the Yorkshire Wildlife Trust and a fairly rare example of a limestone wood. Follow the path downhill to a T-junction of tracks (C), turn right and keep along a broad track, heading downhill all the while. Through the trees there is a fine view ahead over Wharfedale, and soon the river comes into sight. Near the bottom, the track bends sharply to the left and continues down to a road (D).

Turn left along the road for about ¼ mile (0·4 km) and, where the road comes very close to the river (E), turn right over a ladder stile, at a public footpath sign to Grassington Bridge, and follow the path through the trees down to the river-bank. Now comes a splendid finale to the walk as the path keeps along the river-bank all the way up to Grassington Bridge, at first through woods high up above the river and later dropping down and continuing across meadows. At the seventeenth-century bridge (F), turn left onto the road and back to the village.

The peaceful Wharfe upstream from Grassington

25

5 Ingleton waterfalls

Start:	Ingleton
Distance:	4 miles (6·5 km)
Approximate time:	2½ hours
Parking:	Station car park at Ingleton
Refreshments:	Pubs and cafés in Ingleton, two farms *en route*
Ordnance Survey maps:	Landranger 98 (Wensleydale & Upper Wharfedale) and Outdoor Leisure 2 (Yorkshire Dales – Western area)

General description *This is an 'up, across and down' walk: up the narrow, rocky gorge of the River Twiss, across a stretch of open country, and down the even rockier and narrower gorge of the River Doe. It is spectacularly attractive at any time of year, even in bad weather and, although the paths*

are well surfaced, care must be taken as they do get slippery when wet. Although this is a short walk, there is a lot of climbing up and down steps. Most of it is on private land and a modest charge is made.

The narrow streets of Ingleton are dominated by the great Victorian railway viaduct, and it was the railway that brought the first tourists into the area. Now the railway has gone, the viaduct is redundant but the tourists come in ever increasing numbers by car. Ironically the walk begins at the car park on the site of the old railway station.

Drop down to the main street, turn right and then bear left downhill at the waterfalls sign. Cross the two rivers, just above their confluence, and take the first turning on the right **(A)**. This is where the fee is paid at the start of the waterfalls walk.

Continue under an arch, straight ahead through a caravan site and, at the far end of the site, the broad track soon narrows to a path which follows the bank of the River Twiss. A kissing-gate marks the real start of the walk, through a most dramatic, rocky,

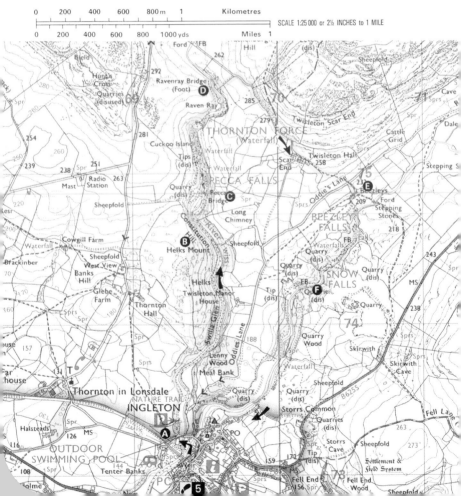

The River Twiss cascades down Pecca Falls

tree-lined gorge, up and down steps and by delightful waterfalls all the way. In a while turn right over a foot-bridge (B) and continue along the opposite bank of the river. At a second footbridge (C), recross the river by the impressive Pecca Falls; the path now climbs up along the edge of these. They look even more impressive seen at close range, as the waters thunder over the rocks. Carry on climbing past a series of foaming cataracts, emerging at the top from the steep-sided gorge into more open country. At this point there is one of the most strategically sited kiosks dispensing drinks and snacks that it is possible to imagine. In a short while you arrive at another impressive fall, Thornton Force, this time a single drop rather than a series of falls. The path continues to the top of the fall and ahead to a third footbridge. Cross over (D), up the steps ahead to a gate, go through and turn right along a wide, walled track.

This track gives panoramic views looking towards Ingleton and the fells beyond, a striking contrast to the narrow, enclosed valley you have just left and the similar one you will shortly enter. Keep ahead over a stile at the first group of buildings, past a farm on the right, over another stile and, with Ingle-

borough dominating the landscape ahead, continue to a lane. Cross over, keep along the tarmac track in front for a few yards and then turn right (E) in front of a farmhouse, along a track that bears left through a metal gate.

Continue to a footpath sign, turning left downhill into a wooded gorge to follow another rocky path through a narrow ravine and up and down steps, this time by the River Doe. Immediately there are a series of spectacular falls: first Beezley Falls, followed by Snow Falls and, at one stage, the path proceeds along the top of an almost perpendicular gorge amidst most attractive woodland; easily the most dramatic section of the entire walk. In a while turn left over a footbridge (F), continue along the other bank of the river and soon the valley begins to widen out and become less sheer.

The path winds through woodland, and on emerging from the trees, the buildings of Ingleton can be seen ahead. Pass through a metal gate, keep ahead along a path above the river, through an abandoned quarry, eventually reaching a metal gate. Here turn right along a lane into Ingleton and walk through the village, past the church, back to the car park.

6 West Burton and Morpeth Gate

Start:	West Burton
Distance:	5 miles (8 km)
Approximate time:	2½ hours
Parking:	By the side of the village green at West Burton
Refreshments:	Pub in West Burton
Ordnance Survey maps:	Landranger 98 (Wensleydale & Upper Wharfedale) and Outdoor Leisure 30 (Yorkshire Dales – Northern & Central areas)

General description *West Burton lies near the junction of Wensleydale and the tributary valleys of Bishopdale and Walden. This modest walk is divided into three almost equal but contrasting sections: first across fields to Aysgarth Church, secondly along the banks of the River Ure past the lower of Aysgarth's series of three falls, before heading towards the remains of a chapel, and thirdly an exhilarating ridge walk back to West Burton, giving glorious views.*

The houses and cottages of West Burton are mainly grouped around the wide, rectangular green and this, coupled with a waterfall just off its north-eastern corner, makes it a particularly charming village. Start by following the road round the green in a clockwise direction through the village and, where it bends to the right, turn left by a gate

(A), squeezing through a gap between buildings, and take the straight path ahead between a fence on the right and a wall on the left. In a few yards descend a short flight of steps, cross a road and, almost directly opposite, go through a gate and down more steps, at a public footpath sign to Eshington Bridge. Proceed straight across the middle of a field, through a gate ahead by the side of a barn, bearing slightly right to a stone stile and yellow waymark in the far right-hand corner of the next field. Climb the stile and keep ahead, with Bishopdale Beck on the left, over another stile and turn right to follow a path across meadows towards a wall ahead. Keeping by the wall on the left, climb a stile and continue ahead, gradually drawing closer to the beck and making for a footpath sign and stone stile straight ahead.

Climb over to join a road **(B)**, turn left over the bridge and look out for a gap in a wall at a public footpath sign for Aysgarth Church. Go through and head uphill across a field towards some steps and a gate. Pass through the gate and turn right to a stile a few yards ahead. Climb over, continue towards a wall on the right, go through a gate and keep ahead to another gate in the far right-hand corner of the field. Go through it and head downhill, by a wire fence on the right, to a stile by a footpath sign. Climb it, head uphill again to a stone stile, over that and continue to a gate and onto a road. Cross over and take the tarmac drive opposite which soon heads downhill. At this point the sound of Aysgarth Falls will be clearly heard and in front is Aysgarth Church.

Enter the churchyard, continue right up to the church porch and then turn sharp right **(C)**, climbing a stone stile just past the church. Keep ahead to another stile, climb it

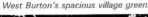

West Burton's spacious village green

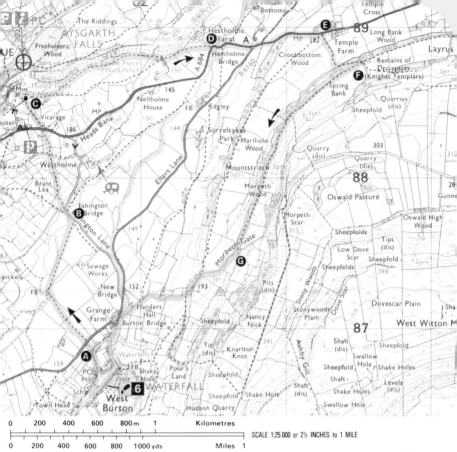

SCALE 1:25 000 or 2½ INCHES to 1 MILE

and enter a small wood, and then continue through the wood to another stile and a public footpath sign at the far end. Climb over and keep ahead towards a wall on the left. Immediately below are Aysgarth Falls, and soon you drop down to join a wire fence on the left just above the River Ure. Now comes a lovely stretch of riverside walking, past the dramatic Lower Force, down some steps, through a gate, over a stile and ahead to a small wood, where the path drops right down to the water's edge. Here turn right, climb a stile at a public footpath sign, continue ahead by the river to a stone stile and gate, pass through it and keep ahead to another stone stile and gate. Go through, continue to a gate and public footpath sign, pass through the gate and bear right, away from the river, heading in a straight line to a stile.

Climb over, turn left along the road **(D)**, cross Hestholme Bridge and continue along the road for ½ mile (0·8 km), climbing quite steeply. Over to the left the towers of Bolton Castle stand out clearly above the dale. Just after the road levels out, turn right **(E)** over a stone stile by two public footpath signs. Follow the left-hand one, to Templar's Chapel, along a broad track, by a wall on the left, across a field and turn sharp left through a

gate, to ascend a wooded ridge. At the top of the ridge, the track bears right and here turn sharp right through a gate **(F)**, at a public footpath sign to Morpeth Gate. Just a few yards' detour through the opposite gate leads to the scanty remains of the Penhill Preceptory. This was a chapel of the Knights Templar, built around 1200, which was suppressed and handed over to the Knights Hospitallers in 1312. The remains, excavated in 1840, are those of the chapel only, as the adjoining residential buildings are still beneath the field, never having been uncovered.

Returning to the route, keep by a wall on the right along the top edge of the wooded ridge, through a gate and over a stone stile. Now there are particularly expansive views up both Wensleydale and Bishopdale. Climb another stone stile, keep ahead to a gate, pass through that and continue ahead, making for and then following a wire fence on the right.

Keep along to a metal gate, go through and turn right **(G)** down a broad track called Morpeth Gate (gate here comes from the Danish word 'gata' meaning street). Follow it as it winds down, through woodland and by farms, to Burton Bridge. Turn left and follow the road back to the village green at West Burton, making a short detour to the left to take a look at Burton Force.

7 Reeth, Arkengarthdale and Grinton

Start:	Reeth
Distance:	5½ miles (8·75 km). Shorter version 3½ miles (5·5 km)
Approximate time:	2½ hours (1½ hours for shorter version)
Parking:	Around the village green at Reeth
Refreshments:	Pubs and cafés in Reeth, pub at Grinton
Ordnance Survey maps:	Landranger 92 (Barnard Castle) and 98 (Wensleydale & Upper Wharfedale) and Outdoor Leisure 30 (Yorkshire Dales – Northern & Central areas)

General description The Swaledale village of Reeth forms the focal point of this walk, the first half of which is up and down a length of Arkengarthdale, most northerly of the Yorkshire Dales. The second half continues across riverside meadows between Reeth and Grinton and the gentler scenery here makes an interesting contrast with the wilder terrain of Arkengarthdale.

Narrow lanes and alleys converge on the spacious, sloping village green of Reeth. This village was once an important centre for the local lead-mining industry, and has a superb situation at the junction of Swaledale and Arkengarthdale. Starting at the village green, with your back to the Black Bull, bear left and walk diagonally across the green, passing the post office on the right and continuing along a lane between houses. At a public footpath sign, bear left along a path, climb a stone stile, keep ahead to go through a gate and across a field towards another stone stile. Climb that, continue a few yards towards a farm and then turn left along the farm track, through a gate and by a wall on the right to a road. Turn right **(A)** along the road for just over ¼ mile (0·4 km) and, soon after the road bends to the left, turn right over a stone stile **(B)**, at a public footpath sign to

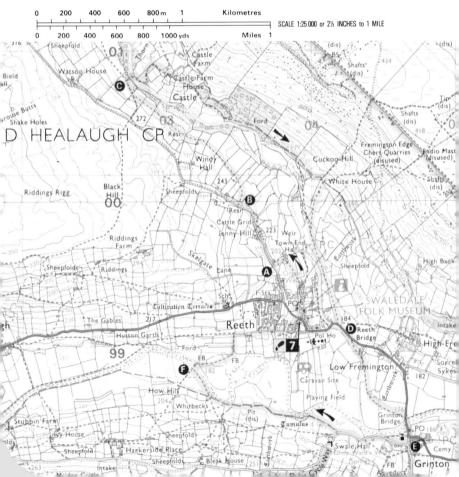

SCALE 1:25 000 or 2½ INCHES to 1 MILE

Reeth stands at the junction of Swaledale and Arkengarthdale

Langthwaite, bearing left across a field towards another stone stile.

The route is now easy to follow as the path, well waymarked, heads across a succession of fields and over a series of stone stiles, keeping roughly parallel with Arkle Beck below on the right and giving fine views up Arkengarthdale. It gradually draws closer to the beck and, on seeing a footbridge below through the trees, bear right down a stony track (C), go through a gate, turn right at a footpath sign, cross the footbridge and turn right at a public footpath sign for Fremington..

The route, still well waymarked, now keeps along the other side of the dale, heading back in the direction of Reeth. After a few yards, turn left at a public footpath sign and head uphill away from the stream. Continue to the top of the rise, go through a gap in a wall and turn right, heading towards a farm. Passing the front of the farm, go through a gate and keep ahead over another succession of stiles. After a while drop down into a wood by the beck, bear slightly left and head uphill, keeping ahead through the trees and out into open country again. In front, the houses of Reeth can be seen. Continue along the path as far as a stile by a metal gate on the right. Climb that, head across a field, keeping to the right of a barn, climb two more stiles and continue along an embankment, parallel to the beck, to a third one. Climb that, keep in a straight line across a field to another stile by a gate, climb that and continue across the next field to reach the main road by Reeth Bridge (D).

Walkers who wish to omit the Grinton section can turn right here, over the bridge and back to Reeth.

Turn left along the road for about 200 yards (184 m) and, at a public bridle-way sign for Grinton, bear right through a gate, along a path by the beck and across meadows, heading towards Grinton. At Grinton Bridge go up some steps and turn right over the bridge into the village. Grinton is an older settlement than Reeth and its mainly fifteenth-century parish church was the only church in Upper Swaledale throughout the Middle Ages, serving a very wide area. Keep past the Bridge Hotel and turn right along a lane (E), signposted Harkerside, by the side of the church.

Follow this lane for just under ½ mile (0·8 km) as far as a sharp left-hand bend. Here bear slightly right, go through a metal gate and along a walled track, keeping along this track by the Swale. The track itself is fairly straight but the river meanders. Where the track joins the river-bank for the second time, continue ahead to the suspension bridge (F), cross it and turn right.

Climb a stile and keep ahead, bearing left over a footbridge, through a gate and up a walled path. Turn right at a footpath sign along another walled track, which heads straight into Reeth. At a sign which says 'Unsuitable for Lorries', turn left for a few yards through a new housing estate, take the first turn on the right and walk along a narrow path which leads directly back to the village green.

8 How Stean Gorge and Upper Nidderdale

Start:	Between Stean and Lofthouse
Distance:	5 miles (8 km)
Approximate time:	2½ hours
Parking:	How Stean car park. Follow signs to Stean from Lofthouse and the car park is on the left just before crossing a stream
Refreshments:	Café at How Stean Gorge, pub at Middlesmoor, pub at Lofthouse
Ordnance Survey maps:	Landranger 99 (Northallerton & Ripon) and Outdoor Leisure 30 (Yorkshire Dales – Northern & Central areas)

General description Despite the construction of reservoirs, Upper Nidderdale possesses some of the wildest and loneliest of Dales scenery. The walk begins by a spectacular gorge, proceeds to a rare example of a hilltop village, continues up one side of the dale and returns along the other side, sometimes by the side of and sometimes just above the narrow, rocky,

How Stean Gorge

infant River Nidd. The short, sharp climb up to Middlesmoor provides the only reasonably strenuous stretch.

Begin by crossing the stream and turning right, following the lane up to the How Stean café and car park entrance. Here you have a choice of either following the route along the lane by the edge of How Stean Gorge or paying a fee to go through the gorge itself, where paths and bridges at different levels allow for a much closer view. How Stean Beck has carved a narrow chasm through the rocks here, up to 70 ft (21 m) deep.

The route keeps along the lane as far as a stone stile and public footpath sign for Middlesmoor. Turn right over this stile (**A**), squeeze through a gap in a fence and keep ahead along a path that soon crosses the stream, giving another fine view of the gorge. Continue up a flight of steps to a gate, go through and head across to a footpath sign by a gap in the wall on the right. Turn left, following yellow waymarks and Nidderdale Way signs, pass through another stone stile and keep ahead by a wall on the left. In front are the cottages and church of Middlesmoor. Climb up towards the village, over a stone stile and through a gap in a wall onto the road. Turn left and follow the road as it curves steeply to the right up to the village. Middlesmoor occupies an unusually exposed, hilltop position, 1,000 ft (305 m) above sea level, and its cottages, pub and church lie huddled together as if for mutual protection against the winter gales.

Follow the road past the village inn and post office and, just after the last building on the right, turn right onto a broad track (**B**) and immediately left, through a gate, to follow a grassy path straight ahead, clipping the corner of a car park wall. Climb a stile, keep by a wall on the left over another stile and continue past the edge of a plantation. Go through a gap, bear right across the middle of a field to a stile, climb over and keep straight ahead. From here there is a superb view down Nidderdale, looking towards Gouthwaite Reservoir. Passing a building on the right, keep ahead to a gap in a wall, go through and across to another gap, through that to yet another gap and here turn right along a track towards a farm. Passing the farm buildings on the right, continue along the track, through a gate and ahead. Go through another gate, keeping by a wall on the right all the time, to a gate at the corner of a plantation. Here turn right, then through another gate and head downhill, bearing left across a small stream, and on to the corner of a wall and wire fence. Climb a stile by a yellow waymark, head down to the bottom left-hand corner of the next field and look out for some rather indistinct stone

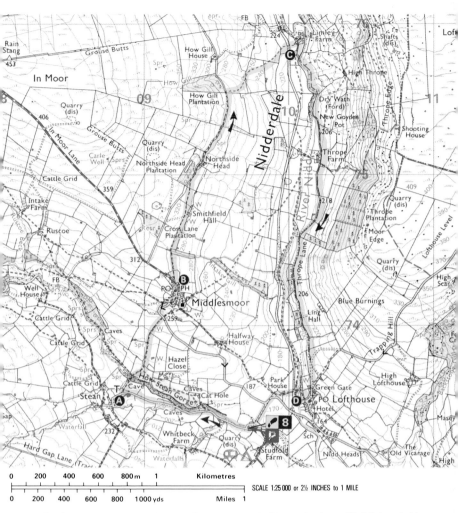

steps. Climb these, continue ahead a few
yards to a much more obvious stile, climb
that and proceed diagonally across the next
field to another stone stile. Climb over and a
gap in the fence ahead leads onto a tarmac
road.

Go straight across, squeeze through
another gap in the fence opposite and keep
ahead towards a farm. Pass through a gap in
a stone wall ahead and turn right onto a track
(C), now following yellow waymarks and
Nidderdale Way signs along a fairly straight
route by the River Nidd to Lofthouse,
1½ miles (2·25 km) away. At this point the
rocky river-bed is often dry. In a short while,
climb a ladder stile and cross to the other
bank of the river. As the Nidd here is narrow
and there are plenty of large slabs, this
should present no problem. The rest of the

way to Lofthouse is along this left-hand side
of the river, mostly about 100 yards (92 m)
from and raised above it, following a partially
walled track called Thrope Lane, which gives
lovely views across the dale. Eventually you
join a narrow road which drops down into
Lofthouse.

In the village centre, where the road bears
left at the war memorial, turn right at the end
of a row of cottages **(D)** along a path which
soon bears left, crosses the river and continues ahead to a road. Cross over, go through a
gate opposite, at a public footpath sign for
Middlesmoor, and keep ahead across a field,
by a wire fence on the left, to a gate and
another road. Continue along this road and,
where it turns right, keep ahead along a
narrow lane to the car park, about 100 yards
(92 m) ahead.

9 Semer Water

Start:	Semer Water
Distance:	6 miles (9·5 km)
Approximate time:	3 hours
Parking:	Parking area by the shore of the lake
Refreshments:	None
Ordnance Survey maps:	Landranger 98 (Wensleydale & Upper Wharfedale) and Outdoor Leisure 30 (Yorkshire Dales – Northern & Central areas)

General description *Semer Water, the only natural lake in the Yorkshire Dales apart from Malham Tarn, is surrounded by moors and thinly populated farmland and, although of modest size, exudes an atmosphere of both mystery and lonely grandeur. This is a short, easy walk that has historic as well as scenic attractions, following the line of a Roman road and passing the ruins of an old church.*

> *Semerwater rise, Semerwater sink,*
> *And swallow all save this li'le house*
> *That gave me meat and drink*

According to legend, it was with these words that an angel disguised as a beggar, who had been refused food in every house bar one, a poor crofter's, cursed the city that stood on the site and caused it to disappear beneath the waters. Hence Semer Water was born and both legend and lonely setting combine to give the lake a definite air of mystery. A more down-to-earth explanation is that the lake originated from the action of glaciers, which gouged out its bed during the Ice Age.

From the parking area by the lakeside, walk along the lane towards the hamlet of Countersett. Cross the bridge over the River Bain, at just over 2½ miles (4 km) long reputedly England's shortest river, and continue uphill to a cross-roads **(A)**. A few yards along the Hawes road turn left, at a public footpath sign for Hawes End, almost immediately going through a gate on the left and heading across a field to the right-hand side of a barn. Here bear left, go through a gate, cross a stream and continue up to another barn. Pass to the left of it and keep ahead to a stone stile in the wall on the left. From here there is a good panoramic view over the lake, encircled by hills and moorland. Carry on uphill, proceeding diagonally across the next field and drawing towards a wall on the left. Keep by that wall, soon climbing a stone stile ahead. Continue

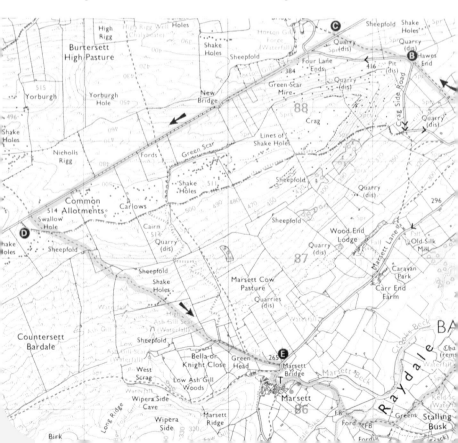

roughly parallel to the wall on the left and, at the top of the hill, join a lane (**B**). Follow it for a short distance to a public footpath sign for Horton Gill Bridge and turn right over a stone stile, to follow the path ahead downhill across rough grass, looking for a gate and stile in the wall in front. Climb over and turn left along a wide, straight, walled track (**C**). This follows the line of a Roman road, built in the first century AD to link the Roman fort at Bainbridge with Ribchester in Lancashire. Keep along this almost geometrically straight route for 1 ½ miles (2·25 km), crossing a lane and climbing, gently but continuously, with superb views on both sides.

On arriving at two public footpath signs (**D**), turn left over a stone stile, at the sign for Marsett, and head straight up the side of the fell towards a small depression near some rocks. Go through a gate, continue across this wild, lonely, but lovely landscape and, at the top of a ridge by a yellow waymark, bear left through a gap in a wall. Keep ahead, veering slightly away from a wall on the right across rough pasture (there is no clear path), heading in the direction of Marsett which can soon be seen at the bottom of the valley. At this point, Semer Water also comes into sight, just over to the left. Head in a straight line towards the village, climb a ladder stile in a wall ahead and then keep by a wall on the

An aura of mystery pervades lonely Semer Water

right, continuing downhill all the while. Climb another wall, continue down to a gate and stone stile, climb that and keep ahead to join a farm track, turning left along it to a road (**E**).

Turn right over Marsett Bridge, left around the edge of the village green and along a track by Marsett Beck. In a while, the track bears right, away from the stream. Follow it over a footbridge and then bear slightly right, away from it, to cross another footbridge ahead. Bear slightly left across one more footbridge, just over 100 yards (92 m) ahead, and turn left by a wall on the right. Look out for a stone stile in that wall, climb it, turn left and keep along the other side of the wall up to a barn. Just past the barn, turn left over a stone stile and take the path ahead across a field, bearing slightly right and heading uphill. Climb another stone stile and keep ahead, passing the right-hand end of a wall and crossing a stream. Continue straight ahead, following yellow waymarks, across several fields and over stiles in the direction of Semer Water. Approaching a water-fall, bear right through a gate, climb a stone stile near a wall corner and keep ahead to the ruined church of Stalling Busk. These scanty remains possess an air of mystery almost as powerful as that of the nearby lake. The church was first built in the early seventeenth century, and rebuilt in the early eighteenth century, but in 1909 it was replaced by a new church, more conveniently sited in the centre of the hamlet.

Keep ahead along the side of the church wall at a public footpath sign for Semer Water, following the path in a fairly straight line over several more stiles down to the lake. Soon after reaching the shores of the lake, climb a stile and veer away from it slightly uphill to a barn, climbing a stile on the left-hand side of the barn. Continue straight ahead across several more fields and over more stone stiles up to a lane (**F**). Turn left and follow the lane back to the parking area.

10 Dentdale

Start:	Dent
Distance:	6 miles (9·5 km)
Approximate time:	3 hours
Parking:	Dent
Refreshments:	Pubs and cafés in Dent, café at Gawthrop
Ordnance Survey maps:	Landranger 98 (Wensleydale & Upper Wharfedale) and Outdoor Leisure 2 (Yorkshire Dales – Western area)

General description *Dentdale is some-what different from the other Yorkshire Dales; softer and gentler with fields separated by hedges instead of the usual drystone walls. At times the landscape is almost reminiscent of southern England, until you lift your eyes to the bare slopes of the high fells that line both sides of the dale, stamping it unmistakably as belonging to the Pennines. This walk contains all the ingredients for a good, varied Dales walk: a climb up a wooded ravine followed by a walk along a green lane, a descent through farms, and a return across lush riverside meadows with, of course, the village of Dent to explore at the end.*

With its whitewashed cottages, cobbled street, medieval church and fine position on a platform above the River Dee, with steep hillsides all round, Dent is a delightfully attractive, unspoilt and remote village. In the seventeenth and eighteenth centuries it was the centre of a local knitting industry and its most famous inhabitant was the geologist Adam Sedgwick, whose father was the vicar.

Take the lane immediately opposite the car park entrance , and go past the village green and straight ahead by the cottages, climbing steadily. At the top of the village, the tarmac lane degenerates into a rough stony track. Follow it for the next ¾ mile (1 km), steeply uphill and through several gates, along the edge of Flinter Gill, a wooded ravine, passing a whole series of small waterfalls. Past the head of the ravine, the path starts to flatten out and continues through more open country. All around are the bare, bleak moorlands that lie between Dent and Ingleton.

Just before reaching the top, go through a gate and, a few yards ahead, turn right at a T-junction along a wide, green, walled track **(A)**. By footpath standards this is virtually of motorway dimensions and gives marvellous views over Dentdale on the right. Keep along this track for nearly 1½ miles (2·25 km) eventually reaching a road **(B)**. Turn right along the road as far as a public footpath sign to Underwood.

0	200	400	600	800 m	1

Kilometres

0	200	400	600	800	1000 yds

Miles 1

SCALE 1:25 000 or 2½ INCHES to 1 MILE

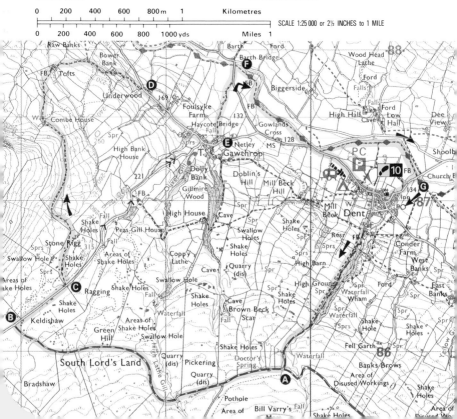

Dent village and church

Here turn left through a gate **(C)** and follow a path ahead across open country, bearing right away from the wall on the left. Passing a rocky outcrop on the right, keep ahead, gradually drawing closer to a wall on the left. Climb a ladder stile in the corner of the wall by a gate, keep ahead parallel to another wall on the left across rough grassland, soon bearing right along a stony path. This path keeps below the brow of the hill on the left and later follows a wall on the right. Follow it down past two ruined farm buildings, bearing right and heading gradually downhill all the while. Continue to a stream and, just to the left of a ford, drop down steeply to the bank, look out for and cross a small footbridge and scramble up the other side. Keep ahead, passing a farmhouse on the left, along a winding track. Go through a gate, past a farm, bear left through another gate, heading downhill to pass through two more gates and onto a lane **(D)**.

Turn right along the lane for ½ mile (0·8 km) into the hamlet of Gawthrop. Where the road begins to head downhill, turn left along a track at a public footpath sign to Barth Bridge **(E)**. Bear right past the corner of a farm building, go through a metal gate and head downhill by the edge of a stream on the left, over three stiles, keeping by a wall on the left after the third one. Look for a small gate in the wall, go through it, turn right and continue by the wall, this time on the right, down to a gap in the wall on the right-hand side of a gate. Pass through it onto a road **(F)**, turning left towards Barth Bridge.

Just before the bridge, turn right down a flight of steps, at a public footpath sign, and follow the bank of the Dee across riverside meadows to Dent, an easy and pleasant finale to the walk. The route is easy to follow, keeping by the river most of the way, across several stiles and footbridges. At one stage the path joins the road for a few yards and you can keep along it to the village but a more attractive and only slightly lengthier approach is to continue along the riverside path, from where there are striking views of the village and church on the right, to Church Bridge **(G)**. Here turn right and walk through the village, past the church and along the cobbled street, back to the car park.

11 Burnsall and Linton

Start:	Burnsall
Distance:	6½ miles (10·25 km)
Approximate time:	3½ hours
Parking:	Riverside car park at Burnsall
Refreshments:	Pubs and cafés at Burnsall, pub at Linton
Ordnance Survey maps:	Landranger 98 (Wensleydale & Upper Wharfedale) and Outdoor Leisure 10 (Yorkshire Dales – Southern area)

General description A splendid and relaxing walk through some of Wharfedale's finest scenery, embracing very pleasant riverside walking, an isolated church, two of the most picturesque Dales villages and extensive views. There is little uphill walking, apart from a gentle climb out of Linton.

With its seventeenth- and eighteenth-century cottages, medieval church, riverside meadows and handsome bridge, Burnsall is a most attractive village and makes a fine walking centre.

Start by taking the riverside path between the Red Lion and the seventeenth-century bridge and follow it through two gates, passing Burnsall Church on the left. The church dates from the fourteenth century, although it was largely rebuilt in the sixteenth, and contains two rare examples of Viking hogback tombs along with some even rarer, if fragmentary, Saxon sculptures. Nearby is the building of the old grammar school, founded in 1602, which is now appropriately used as the local primary school.

The path hugs the river-bank all the way, passing through a gorge opposite the limestone cliff of Loup Scar. Continue to a suspension bridge **(A)**, cross the river and turn left along the other bank. After about a mile (1·5 km), go through a gate where the valley broadens out and bear slightly away from the river, heading in the direction of Linton Church, clearly visible on the other side of the Wharfe. Near the corner of a stone wall, bear right over a stile to join a broad track and follow this past Grassington Old Mill (now a private residence) and along a tarmac lane for about 100 yards (92 m). Turn left at a public footpath sign to Grassington Bridge to rejoin the riverside path and keep ahead, going through three gaps in walls to a footbridge **(B)**.

SCALE 1:25 000 or 2½ INCHES to 1 MILE

Turn left over this bridge (nicknamed the Tin Bridge), bear right, then left and climb some steps to a lane. Turn left along the lane to take a closer look at Linton Church, an unpretentious but delightful little church, dating from the late twelfth century but mostly rebuilt in the fifteenth. The most surprising feature is its isolated position above the river. This is because it serves four parishes – Grassington, Hebden, Linton and Threshfield – and is situated roughly equidistant from each.

Retracing your steps from the church, turn left along a track by the side of the house on the left (C) and, after a few yards, right through a gate to take a path between a wall on the right and wire fence on the left. At the road turn right, soon bearing left to follow it into Linton. Linton is one of the most idyllic of Dales villages with a large green, a stream crossed by ancient footbridges, stone cottages and, unusually in such a small and comparatively remote place, an elegant and ornate classical building, which lines one side of the green. This is the Fountaine Hospital, founded in 1721 by a local benefactor, Richard Fountaine, as almshouses for 'six poor men or women'. It is thought that the building may have been designed by the distinguished architect Sir John Vanbrugh.

In the village turn first left (D), with the

The idyllic village of Linton

stream on your right, and keep ahead past cottages and farms, turning left along a walled track by the last farm. Follow the track uphill, over a stile and ahead, keeping by the wall on the left all the time. Climb a ladder stile at a public footpath sign and, bearing slightly left, continue uphill across a field towards the left-hand edge of a line of trees in front. With the greater altitude come superb views over Grassington and Wharfedale for the next mile (1·5 km). Continue past the end of the trees, keeping by a wall on the right, to a stone stile.

Climb the stile, turn left along the narrow, walled lane (E) and, at a T-junction, turn right to drop down into the secluded hamlet of Thorpe. At the bottom of the hill, bear left uphill (F) along another narrow lane.

At the top of the hill where the lane bends to the left, turn right through a gate (G) (public footpath sign to Burnsall) along a walled track which, as it winds downhill, gives more fine views over Wharfedale. Where the track ends, climb a ladder stile on the right and head downhill to a gate in a fence by the edge of some trees. Go through the gate and, following footpath signs, bear left parallel to a curving wall on the left, to a gate in the wall. Go through this gate, cross a beck and keep ahead, climbing gently to another gate in a wall in front. Pass through and keep ahead across the next field to another gate, pass through that and continue just above a line of trees on the left, gradually bearing downhill to a public footpath sign by a wall.

Turn right here, keeping the wall on your left, pass through a gate, cross a narrow lane, and go through the opposite gate (public footpath sign to Burnsall). Keep ahead to go over the brow of the hill, from where there is an excellent view of the church and village of Burnsall in front. Go through a gate in a wall and turn right, heading downhill to a stone stile in the corner of a wall. Keep going in a straight line over a succession of these stone stiles, heading back to Burnsall. On reaching the village, pass through three gates onto the road. Turn right down the village street to the bridge, river and car park.

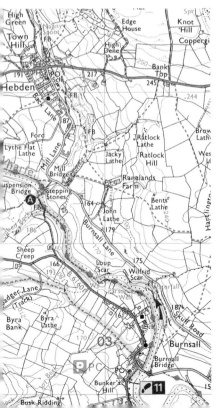

12 Ribblehead and Chapel le Dale

Start:	Ribblehead
Distance:	7 miles (11·25 km)
Approximate time:	3½ hours
Parking:	Opposite Station Inn at Ribblehead
Refreshments:	Pub at Ribblehead, Old Hill Inn near Chapel le Dale
Ordnance Survey maps:	Landranger 98 (Wensleydale & Upper Wharfedale) and Outdoor Leisure 2 (Yorkshire Dales – Western area)

General description *The building of the Settle – Carlisle railway is the thread running through this undemanding though spectacular walk, amidst the dramatic countryside of the 'Three Peaks' of Whernside, Ingleborough and Pen-y-ghent. In addition to these natural phenomena, the route is dominated for most of the way by the almost equally dramatic man-made structure of Ribblehead Viaduct. As well as being a major triumph of Victorian railway engineering, the viaduct blends in with its wild and bare surroundings so perfectly that it seems almost to be part of the landscape and even, it could be argued, to enhance it.*

Take the broad track by the side of the Station Inn which heads across rough grassland towards the viaduct. Immediately there is a striking view of the viaduct, backed by the slopes of Whernside. The sight of a steam train chugging across it is even more dramatic and is guaranteed to attract an army of rail enthusiasts lying in wait with cameras poised.

Ribblehead Viaduct is the most impressive structure on the Settle – Carlisle line, which was built between 1869 and 1875 as part of a new route from London to Scotland, the last main line to be constructed during the Victorian railway era. Here, between the heads of the Ribble, Ure and Eden valleys, it crosses some of the wildest and most inhospitable Pennine moorland and the physical and organisational problems of construction, plus the human cost, were immense.

Follow the track under the massive arches of the viaduct **(A)** (¼ mile (0·4 km) long, with a maximum height of 106 ft (32 m), keep ahead through a gate and on past farm buildings to a footbridge over Waterscales Beck.

Cross the bridge **(B)**, turn left through a

gate along a tarmac farm road and pass through several more gates, eventually bearing left to join another farm road. Cross the beck again and continue ahead to a gate by the side of a cattle grid. At this point there is a superb view of Ingleborough directly ahead.

Bear right, away from the road, at a public bridle-way sign to Philpin Lane, across the grass to a gate. Pass through, keep ahead by a wall on the left and, at the corner of the wall, continue across the usually dry bed of the stream in front of you to a ladder stile. By now the landscape has changed, gradually but noticeably, from the bleak, bare, open moorland around Ribblehead to neat green fields, criss-crossed by stone walls, with a few trees dotted around. Climb the ladder stile and keep ahead, veering slightly to the left to a gate. Go through, continuing along a narrow rocky path to a farm road, and turn left along it to the Ingleton – Hawes road **(C)**.

At the road turn right (Old Hill Inn is a few

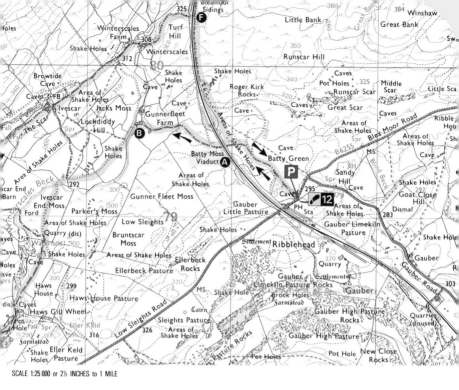

SCALE 1:25 000 or 2½ INCHES to 1 MILE

yards to the left) down into the hamlet of Chapel le Dale, turning right along a lane **(D)** and over a stream to the church. It was to this tiny building that the bodies of navvies killed during the construction of the railway, plus those of women and children who died in the appalling conditions of the shanty towns, were brought for burial. It has been estimated that over 200 bodies lie in unmarked graves in the churchyard, and inside the church is a memorial to all who lost their lives in the building of the Settle – Carlisle railway.

Turn right up the narrow lane in front of the church, continue through a gate (passing Hurtle Pot on the right) and, where the lane ends, keep ahead along a broad track (signposted to Ellerbeck) through a most attractive rocky, tree-lined gorge. Passing a rather strange, futuristic bronze statue of a man (placed here after having been retrieved from Hurtle Pot), continue up into open country.

Bear right across a beck **(E)**, at a public footpath sign to Deepdale, and follow the track past farm buildings, veering right to a gate. Pass through and keep along the clear, wide track, past several farms and through a series of gates, following the lower slopes of Whernside. From the track there are superb views over the dale towards the viaduct. After 1½ miles (2·25 km) at the point where the track bends sharply to the left, keep ahead a few yards to a stile (public bridle-way sign to Winterscales), climb it and continue ahead past more farms and through another succession of gates, keeping in a roughly straight line. Soon you get a fine view on the right of the third of the 'Three Peaks' – Pen-y-ghent – unseen up till now. At the second footbridge (by a group of farm buildings), keep ahead along a stony track to a gate, go through and bear left, following a stream, towards Blea Moor signal-box.

Bear right under the railway bridge and turn right **(F)** to pick up a track running parallel to the railway. For the final stretch of the walk, keep by the railway, heading across rough grassland to meet the broad, well surfaced track which leads back to the Station Inn and car park.

Grandeur both natural and man-made – Ribblehead Viaduct backed by Whernside

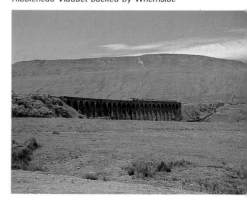

41

13 Cam Head

Start:	Kettlewell
Distance:	5½ miles (8·75 km)
Approximate time:	3 hours
Parking:	Kettlewell
Refreshments:	Pubs and cafés in Kettlewell, pub at Starbotton
Ordnance Survey maps:	Landranger 98 (Wensleydale & Upper Wharfedale) and Outdoor Leisure 30 (Yorkshire Dales – Northern & Central areas)

General description A steady but fairly easy climb from Kettlewell to Cam Head along a walled green lane is followed by a winding descent down another green lane into the small village of Starbotton. Whether ascending or descending, the views over Wharfedale are both superb and extensive. The return to Kettlewell is an easy and pleasant walk across meadows bordering the River Wharfe.

Like many villages in the Yorkshire Dales, Kettlewell started as a small farming community and later expanded with the creation first of textile and later of lead-mining industries in the area. Many of its houses and cottages belong to the heyday of those industries in the eighteenth and nineteenth centuries, including the Victorian church.

Start by turning left out of the car park and, where the main road turns left, keep ahead past cottages. Turn left by the village

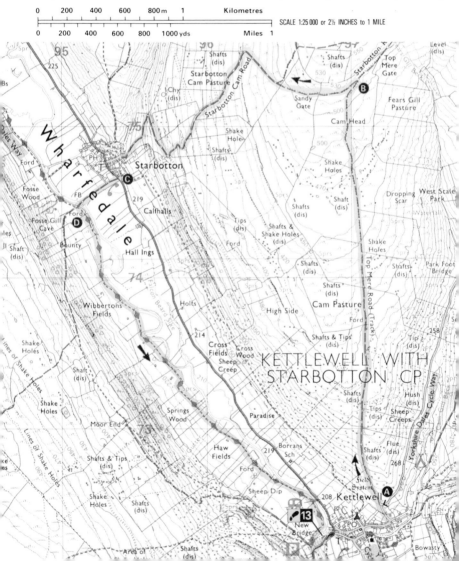

The path to Cam Head gives glorious views over Kettlewell and Wharfedale

maypole, signposted to Leyburn, left again to cross the bridge over Dowber Gill Beck and turn right at another Leyburn sign. Follow the road around a sharp left-hand bend steeply uphill and, where it does an equally sharp right-hand bend, keep straight ahead along a wide, walled track at a public bridle-way sign to Cam Head **(A)**.

This track, called Top Mere Road, climbs steadily but not steeply (in fact the steepest part comes before you leave the road), through three gates and past the remains of lead-mine workings, for just over 1 ½ miles (2·25 km) to Cam Head. As you climb, the ever changing views all around are a delight. Behind are the houses of Kettlewell huddled below, while beyond the village the smooth, bright green, walled fields slope gently to the river, with belts of woodland adorning the higher slopes and, above them, the bare limestone uplands stretching away in the distance. To the left are the rugged slopes separating Wharfedale from Littondale and to the right the landscape is dominated by the austerely beautiful flanks of Great Whernside. In front the steadily ascending green lane continues towards Cam Head.

After passing through the third gate, you leave the walled track and continue across open country to the top of Cam Head. Ahead is Tor Dike, an ancient earthwork that stretches for over ½ mile (0·8 km) across a limestone ridge, making use of the natural

defence provided by that ridge. It is thought to have been constructed in the first century AD by the local native tribes, to withstand the Roman invasion.

At the top, turn sharp left, at a public footpath sign to Starbotton **(B)**, and keep ahead to climb two ladder stiles and begin the descent into Wharfedale. After the second stile you join another walled track, Starbotton Cam Road, which you follow for about 1 ¼ miles (2 km) into the village. The track twists and turns sharply, giving more outstanding views, especially looking ahead to Upper Wharfedale and the slopes of Langstrothdale Chase. After passing through a gate, the track bends sharply to the left and drops down to the attractive, random collection of farms and cottages that make up Starbotton.

Turn left at the road and, at a public footpath sign to Arncliffe, Kettlewell and Buckden **(C)**, turn right through a gate and along a path that leads down to a foot-bridge over the River Wharfe. Cross the bridge and turn left over a stone stile at a public footpath sign for Kettlewell **(D)**.

The remainder of the route is along a delightful path across the meadows bordering the Wharfe, over a succession of stiles, up to Kettlewell Bridge, a distance of about 1 ¾ miles (2·5 km). By the bridge go through a gate and turn left over the river back to the car park.

14 Aysgarth Falls and Bolton Castle

Start:	Aysgarth Falls
Distance:	6½ miles (10·25 km)
Approximate time:	3½ hours
Parking:	National Park car park at Aysgarth Falls
Refreshments:	Café at Aysgarth Falls, restaurant at Bolton Castle, pub at Carperby
Ordnance Survey maps:	Landranger 98 (Wensleydale & Upper Wharfedale) and Outdoor Leisure 30 (Yorkshire Dales – Northern & Central areas)

General description *Wide and extensive vistas are a constant feature of this most varied and scenic walk, which starts at a series of spectacular falls and continues to the ruins of Bolton Castle, whose walls stand high up above Wensleydale and are in view throughout a large proportion of the way. An ideal time to do this walk is on a clear day after heavy rain, when the scenery can be enjoyed at its best and the falls can be seen at their most majestic, in full spate.*

There are three waterfalls in succession at Aysgarth, extending along a ¾ mile- (1 km-) stretch of the River Ure. The first to be visited is Upper Force, reached by taking the signposted path at the far end of the car park, which winds through woods, beside a short stretch of road and through a gate up to the edge of the falls, backed by steep wooded banks.

Return to the gate, go through and turn left along the road. On the other side of Aysgarth Bridge is a former mill which now houses a coach and carriage museum. At a footpath sign for Middle and Lower Force, turn right through a gate (**A**) and follow a path through Freeholder's Wood (so-called because local freeholders still retain common rights in it) down to Middle Force, where an observation platform has been constructed. It is an impressive sight, with the view of the great cascade of water below enhanced by the tower of Aysgarth Church on the hill above. Continue along the woodland path, through a gate, across a meadow and through another gate, dropping down into the riverside woods again to view Lower Force.

From here the route to Bolton Castle is easy to follow, with plenty of signposts and yellow waymarks all the way. A few yards past Lower Force, turn left over a stile to leave the river and head across the field towards a fence, turning right by that fence and continuing through a gap in the wall ahead. Keep ahead across the next field, veer slightly left to a gate, pass through it and along a path towards a farm, going through another gate and turning right through the farmyard. Pass the back of the farmhouse and continue along a track. Here views up and down Wensleydale start to open up and, for the first time, the towers of Bolton Castle can be seen in the distance.

After a few yards bear right, away from the track, keeping by a wire fence on the right and, at a wall, turn right over a stone stile and continue across the middle of the next field in the direction of a large group of farm buildings. On reaching a wall, bear right over a stile and keep ahead over another stile, through a gap in a wall and ahead, by a wall on the right. At the corner of that wall, keep straight ahead towards a wall and line of trees in front (**B**). Here take the path along the left-hand side of the wall, over a stile and continue ahead, following a green lane lined for the most part with hedges for the next ¾ mile (1 km). This is an ancient routeway called Thoresby Lane and, just off the lane, some mounds in a field are all that remains of the Danish settlement of Thoresby, deserted some time in the Middle Ages.

Near the end of this green lane a farm is passed and, about 100 yards (92 m) further on, bear left over a foot-bridge, turn left through a gap in a fence, keep ahead over a low wall and, ignoring the ladder stile in front, turn right. Now head across a field towards a barn at the far end, pass through a gap in the wall to the right of that barn and keep straight across the next field to a gap in the wall alongside a metal gate. Go through onto a lane (**C**) and follow it for ½ mile (0·8 km) up to the village of Castle Bolton (**D**).

As you walk up the lane, the high walls of Bolton Castle look both forbidding and impenetrable, but this is somewhat misleading, as Bolton was one of the later medieval castles, built for residential as much as military purposes towards the end· of the fourteenth century by Sir Richard le Scrope, Lord Chancellor to Richard II. It comprises rectangular curtain walls three storeys high, with a tower in each corner. Grouped around the four walls are the remains of the various domestic buildings: storehouses, stables, bakehouse and brewery on the ground floor; kitchens, living quarters and chapel on the upper floors. Two rooms to particularly look out for are the dungeon, a suitably dark and grim cellar into which prisoners were dropped through a gap in the roof (now complete with frightening audio-visual effects), and Mary's Room on the second floor of the south-west tower. Mary Queen of Scots spent almost a year of her long captivity in England here,

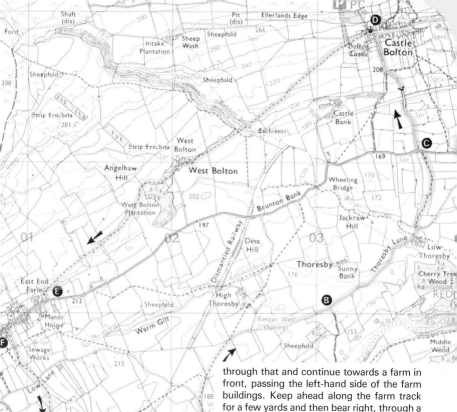

SCALE 1:25 000 or 2½ INCHES to 1 MILE

although it is unlikely that the room she used is the so-called Mary's Room. The north-west tower is a bar and restaurant, conveniently located at the half-way stage of the walk. The village of Castle Bolton lies huddled beneath the castle walls, comprising one street of farmhouses and cottages and a tiny medieval church; it is totally uncommercialised and unspoilt, pleasantly old-fashioned and the views from it over Wensleydale are striking.

To continue the walk, take the tarmac lane past the castle and small car park, climb a stile into a field and bear left, making for a stile near the corner of a wall, by yellow waymarks. Climb over, head across to another stile, climb that and keep ahead to the end of the wall. Then bear left across the middle of the field and head down to two metal gates side by side. Pass through the lower one and walk across a field, veering left to a stile, climb over, cross a footbridge and bear right uphill to a gap in a wall. Go through, keep ahead to a metal gate, pass

through that and continue towards a farm in front, passing the left-hand side of the farm buildings. Keep ahead along the farm track for a few yards and then bear right, through a gap in a wall, at a public footpath sign. Pass through another gap in a wall ahead, follow the boundary wall of a plantation on the left to a stile, climb over and keep ahead, crossing a stream and making for a gate. Go through and keep ahead across fields, first through a metal gate and then through a gap in the wall, to enter a field with a number of mounds. Here pick up a track which bears left downhill, through a gate and on through a farmyard to a lane (E). Turn right and follow the lane into the village of Carperby, formerly an important centre of the Quaker movement, its major building a fine, classical, nineteenth-century Meeting House.

Opposite the Wheatsheaf, turn left through a gate (F), at a public footpath sign, into a narrow field, cross a small stream and, a few yards further on, go right through a metal gate. Immediately turn left and follow a straight path, by a wall on the left, across several fields to a lane. Cross over and take the path opposite across a field, keeping by a wall on the right. At a public footpath sign, go through a gap in the wall, bear left and then follow a path in a more or less straight line diagonally across four fields. After the last field, you enter a small wood and bear right at a junction of paths, immediately turning left to head down between the trees and through a gate onto a road. Turn left under a bridge and the first turn on the right leads back to Aysgarth Falls car park.

45

15 All the wonders of Malham

Start:	Malham
Distance:	6 ½ miles (10·25 km)
Approximate time:	3 ½ hours
Parking:	Malham
Refreshments:	Cafés and pub at Malham
Ordnance Survey maps:	Landranger 98 (Wensleydale & Upper Wharfedale) and Outdoor Leisure 10 (Yorkshire Dales – Southern area)

General description *This classic walk encompasses all the scenic and geological wonders that surround the village of Malham – first the wooded ravine and cascading fall of Janet's Foss, secondly the forbidding and spectacular chasm of Gordale Scar, thirdly the peaceful waters of Malham Tarn, fourthly the Water Sinks (where the infant River Aire suddenly disappears), fifthly the dry Watlowes Valley and, last and most dramatic of all, the great natural amphitheatre of Malham Cove. The route is fairly easy but does involve a short, steep scramble up the rocks at the side of Gordale Scar.*

The spectacular limestone scenery around Malham attracts thousands of visitors each year to this otherwise unremarkable but small and pleasant village on the River Aire, with its eighteenth-century cottages and farmhouses. From the car park turn left along the road, right over a footbridge to cross the River Aire **(A)** and right again along a broad path. Climb a stile and follow the very clear, easy, well waymarked footpath to Janet's Foss, a distance of about a mile (1·5 km). The path keeps by the river for most of the way, crossing several ladder stiles. After the last stile, a narrow valley is entered and, soon after, the valley narrows further, almost to a gorge. A gate admits you to the National Trust area of Janet's Foss and the next

The natural amphitheatre of Malham Cove

¼ mile (0·4 km) is particularly attractive as the path follows the rocky wooded gorge up to the impressive waterfall.

Continue along the path that climbs up by the side of the fall, go through a gate and turn right along a lane **(B)**. After 100 yards (92 m), turn left through a gate, at a public footpath sign to Gordale Scar, and follow another broad, well constructed path right up to the foot of the massive and awesome chasm. Gordale Scar was formed by great torrents of melt-water during the Ice Age, about 12,000 to 15,000 years ago, and through it plunges a narrow beck between overhanging cliffs that rise to 300 ft (91·5 m).

On entering the jaws of the scar, it looks as if it is a cul-de-sac ahead but, from the bottom of the fall, a path can be seen which climbs steeply and which initially involves some rough scrambling. In a while, continue up some steps and then along a rocky path. At the top of the gorge, keep ahead over a ladder stile, at a public footpath sign for Malham Tarn, and continue across a marvellously austere and rocky landscape, along the edge of a limestone pavement for most of the way. Gradually draw closer to a stone wall on the left and, in the corner of that wall, climb a ladder stile and turn right to arrive at Street Gate **(C)**, the junction of two ancient and important trans-Pennine routeways, the north – south route from Arncliffe to Malham and the east – west route from Wharfedale to Ribblesdale. Keep ahead along a tarmac track by a wall on the right and, just before a gate and cattle-grid, turn left and follow another wall on the right that forms the boundary of a small plantation. Keep in a straight line parallel with the wall and, shortly after a diversion to the left around another small plantation, a broad track is reached **(D)**. Ahead and to the right lies Malham Tarn, over 1,200 ft (366 m) above sea level, covering 153 acres. It is one of only two natural lakes in the Yorkshire Dales, the other being Semer Water.

Cross over the track and bear left across rough grass, making for the corner of a wall and a wood. At the corner keep ahead in a straight line to the road. Here turn right, cross Malham Beck and then turn immediately left **(E)** through a gate at a public bridle-way sign. Head across to a signpost, bearing left where the sign indicates Water Sinks and Malham Cove. The path makes for the beck and follows it for a few yards, when the beck suddenly disappears underground, reappearing at Aire Head.

Now keep ahead by a wall on the left, gradually dropping down into the dry Watlowes Valley where the path becomes very stony. Keep ahead through the narrow valley with almost perpendicular cliffs both

SCALE 1:25 000 or 2½ INCHES to 1 MILE

sides. The path twists and turns and, at one point turns sharply left, by a public footpath sign, then it goes over a stile and continues downhill. Eventually it levels out and rejoins a wall on the left. Emerging from this narrow valley, climb a ladder stile and, a few yards ahead, is the top of Malham Cove, the climax of the walk (F). Turn right along the top of this great 220 ft- (67 m-) high cliff, across the limestone pavement, with the flat blocks, or clints, separated almost geometrically by the deep narrow crevices, or grikes, in between. The views from here are superb but great care must be taken; in wet weather the slabs become very slippery and an ankle could easily be broken if you stepped by mistake into one of the grikes.

After crossing the top of the cove, climb a ladder stile and turn sharp left to take a stepped path that leads downhill to its base. At the bottom of the steps, detour slightly to the left for a closer inspection of the cove, otherwise turn right through a gate and follow the path by the side of Malham Beck up to the road just above Malham village. At the road, turn left through the village and back to the car park.

16 Sedbergh and Winder

Start: Sedbergh

Distance: 6½ miles (10·25 km)

Approximate time: 3½ hours

Parking: Car park near the church in Sedbergh

Refreshments: Pubs and cafés in Sedbergh

Ordnance Survey maps: Landranger 97 (Kendal & Morecambe) and Pathfinder SD 69/79 617 (Sedbergh and Baugh Fell)

General description *Creating a 'bridge' between the Pennines and the Cumbrian mountains are the Howgills, which rise immediately behind Sedbergh. Their smooth, grassy, rounded slopes provide both excellent walking and dramatic scenery and*

this walk ascends Winder, the most accessible of the Howgill peaks. After descending, the walk finishes off with a relaxing stroll along the banks of the very attractive River Rawthey. Despite being in Cumbria, this area is still within the Yorkshire Dales National Park, forming its north-western fringes.

From almost any point in the narrow streets of Sedbergh, the Howgills can be seen, their steep slopes making a dramatic backcloth on the north side of the town. It is an attractive old town and its principal buildings are the solid medieval church in the centre and the conglomeration of buildings that make up the public school, originally founded as a chantry school in 1525 and now occupying a large area on the town's southern fringes. There are several car parks; the walk begins at the one near the church and library.

Start by walking past the church, turn left at the post office and then right along the road that is signposted to Howgill. Follow this road round to the left and keep along it as

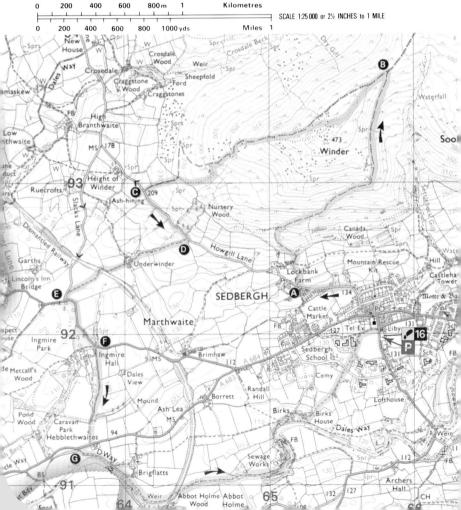

SCALE 1:25 000 or 2½ INCHES to 1 MILE

The smooth slopes of the Howgills rise abruptly behind Sedbergh

far as a public footpath sign to the Fell (**A**). Here turn right onto a broad track and immediately in front are the Howgills, rising abruptly above the valley.

Walk up to the farm, go through a metal gate ahead, continue along a walled track and through another metal gate to gain access to the open fellside. Turn left, keeping by the wall on the left and there is a fine view over to the left of the town nestling among high fells. Just after passing a small wood on the left, bear right, away from the wall and follow a grassy track straight up the open fellside. On reaching a crossing of green tracks just above a ridge, turn right to follow the track that climbs up the side of Winder, giving dramatic views all the way. Keep ahead, climbing steadily and gently, bearing left to reach a cairn. Continue past the cairn, above the steep narrow valley of Settlebeck Gill on the right, and after almost a mile (1·5 km) the path joins a main track coming in from the left near another, smaller cairn (**B**). At this point there is a glorious view ahead of the smooth, steep-sided flanks of Brantfell.

Turn sharp left along this track and follow it over the summit of Winder, from where there are more magnificent panoramic views. At the summit cairn, keep straight ahead along a path that gradually descends towards a small group of trees. Just before the trees, the path swings to the right, shortly afterwards passes through a metal gate and continues down to a lane (**C**). Turn left along this lane and, at the end of the trees on the left, turn right (**D**) over a stile and along the edge of a field, keeping at first by a wall and later a wire fence on the right. Go through a gate and keep ahead, with a stream on the right, through two more gates to a farm. Continue along the farm track and over the

bridge of a disused railway to a lane. Turn left and, in a few yards, left again to join a main road (**E**). Where the road curves to the left, keep ahead, at a public bridle-way sign to the A683 (**F**), along a most pleasant, tree-lined track, following the wall of Ingmire Hall on the right. At the A683, turn right for about 100 yards (92 m), then turn left at a public footpath sign for Birks Mill (**G**), climb a stile and continue to another stile. Climb over that and keep ahead above the River Rawthey on the right.

The next stage of the walk is particularly attractive, as the path keeps close to the thickly wooded riverbank. Climb a stile and keep ahead across riverside meadows, passing Brigflatts on the left, an early centre of the Quaker movement with a Meeting House dating from 1675, the oldest in the North of England. At a disused railway bridge, climb a stile, bear left up the embankment, down the other side and over another stile to rejoin the riverside path, keeping by the river to Birks Mill. At the mill, do not cross the footbridge but keep ahead along a tarmac lane through the hamlet, turning right through a gate at a public footpath sign for the Rawthey Way.

Follow the path along the edge of a field, soon heading down to a stile. Bear left over the stile away from the river, keeping by a wall on the left and climb a ladder stile over that wall. Now bear right, heading towards the far corner of the field in the direction of the school buildings, pass through a gate and keep ahead along a broad path to a gate and road. Go straight across, through the gate opposite and continue along a grassy path, between the buildings of Sedbergh School, up to another gate. Pass through that, keep straight ahead along a tarmac path to a junction, and here bear right, past the church and back to the car park.

17 Burnsall, Trollers Gill and Appletreewick

Start:	Burnsall
Distance:	7 miles (11·25 km)
Approximate time:	3½ hours
Parking:	Riverside car park at Burnsall
Refreshments:	Café and pub at Burnsall, pubs in Appletreewick
Ordnance Survey maps:	Landranger 98 (Wensleydale & Upper Wharfedale), 99 (Northallerton & Ripon) and 104 (Leeds, Bradford & Harrogate), Outdoor Leisure 10 (Yorkshire Dales – Southern area)

General description *Two villages, breezy and open moorland, a spectacular ravine and lush riverside meadows all combine to make an unusually pleasant and varied walk over country that lies between Wharfedale and Nidderdale. There is just one climb, which though fairly lengthy is gradual and easy.*

From the car park in Burnsall, turn right over the bridge and along the lane towards Appletreewick. Walk through the hamlet of Hartlington, cross a stream and, shortly afterwards, turn left over a stile, at a public bridle-way sign for New Road (**A**). Follow an uphill track ahead which gives some splendid walking, being wide, with a springy grass surface and marked with regular footpath signs, and with fine views behind over Burnsall and Wharfedale. Keep ahead all the time, ignoring all footpath signs to right and left and, after the third gate, you emerge onto open moorland. A few yards in front, bear left along another clear, broad track, following bridle-way signs across the moorland, with panoramic views looking towards Upper Nidderdale ahead.

On reaching a road, turn left (**B**), follow the road around a sharp right-hand bend and immediately turn right over a ladder stile, at a public footpath sign for Skyreholme. There is no clear path here across the rough grass but, after bearing slightly left, keep straight ahead, in the direction of the footpath sign, heading downhill into a small valley and keeping by the right-hand side of a stream. Passing a cave called Hell Hole, join a clear track about 100 yards (92 m) ahead and follow it as it winds down through a narrow dry valley. The track later joins a stream on the left and upstream of this is the almost perpendicular limestone ravine of Trollers Gill (there is no public access but it can be seen from the track).

SCALE 1:25 000 or 2½ INCHES to 1 MILE

A glimpse into the limestone ravine of Trollers Gill

Keep ahead to climb a stile and follow the right-hand side of the stream along a most attractive, winding, tree-lined path. Continue over stiles and through gates down to a lane by a bridge (C). Over the bridge to the left is the entrance to Parcevall Hall Gardens, open to the public.

Turn right along this lane, keeping right at the next junction (D) and following another narrow lane for one mile (1·5 km) to Appletreewick, passing through the tiny hamlet of Skyreholme on the way. After a side road on the right, Wharfedale comes into view and, just past the next road junction, you enter Appletreewick. The village is small, quiet but attractive, with a tiny, plain nineteenth-century church and a number of fine houses lining its only street.

Continue through the village and turn left, at a public footpath sign (E), along a walled path that leads down to the River Wharfe. Now turn right onto the riverside path and follow it back to Burnsall. The path is well waymarked and keeps close to the river-bank all the way, apart from one section where it cuts across the neck of a loop in the river. On reaching the road, turn left back over Burnsall Bridge into the village.

18 Kettlewell and Arncliffe

Start:	Kettlewell
Distance:	6 miles (9.5 km)
Approximate time:	3½ hours
Parking:	Kettlewell
Refreshments:	Pubs and cafés in Kettlewell, pub and café at Arncliffe
Ordnance Survey maps:	Landranger 98 (Wensleydale & Upper Wharfedale), Outdoor Leisure 10 (Yorkshire Dales – Southern area) and 30 (Yorkshire Dales – Northern & Central areas)

General description Two dales are included in this walk, which starts from Kettlewell in Wharfedale and climbs steeply across rugged moorland, to drop down into Littondale at the picturesque village of Arncliffe. Then comes a stretch of easy riverside walking by the Skirfare, before returning to Kettlewell over the shoulder of Knipe Scar. Two fairly energetic climbs reward you with magnificent views over both dales.

Kettlewell lies on the banks of the Wharfe, surrounded by steep hillsides and moorlands criss-crossed by drystone walls. Moorland and riverside paths radiate from it, giving walkers an excellent choice of routes. This walk starts by crossing the bridge and keeping straight ahead, through a gate and along a stony walled track, at a public footpath sign for Arncliffe. After a few yards, turn left off the main track, at another public footpath sign, following a path uphill to a ladder stile. Climb over and keep ahead, climbing quite steeply towards the scar in front. Squeeze through the narrow gap in the rocks, to emerge onto an open plateau, and follow yellow waymarks to a footpath sign. Continue ahead in a straight line, enjoying the grand views up Wharfedale on the right. At this stage the path is not very clear but the yellow waymarks indicate the route.

Bear slightly to the right, making for a ladder stile in a wall on the right, climb over, turn left and keep ahead, now following the wall on the left. Soon the path begins to bear slightly to the right, away from the wall and you keep ahead, more or less in a straight line, still following yellow waymarks and climbing steadily all the while. Head towards some more crags in front and, after climbing those, continue to a wall and ladder stile about 200 yards (184 m) ahead. Climb over and bear slightly right to another wall and ladder stile.

0   200   400   600   800 m   1   Kilometres

SCALE 1:25 000 or 2½ INCHES to 1 MILE

0   200   400   600   800   1000 yds   Miles   1

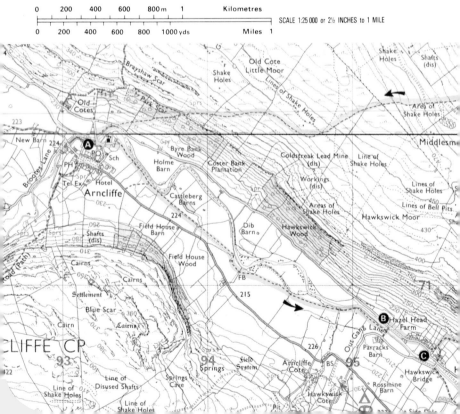

The church and the River Skirfare at Arncliffe

Climb over that and bear left, now heading downhill, with fine views over Littondale, along a green path between heather, bearing slightly right at a footpath sign. Continue down to a gap in a wall, keep straight ahead to the next wall and ladder stile, climb over and continue down to the next wall on the edge of a wood. Here turn left over a ladder stile, turning immediately left and then right to drop sharply down through the wood along a rocky path. Now come superb views of Arncliffe below, backed by steep hills and bare moorlands. At the bottom edge of the wood, go through a gate and continue along a path downhill to a wall and ladder stile. Climb over, head down to a gap in a wall and on to a lane. Cross over, go down some steps and take the riverside path, with Arncliffe church on the left, up to a bridge. Cross the bridge into the village (**A**).

Arncliffe is a gem of a village, well worth exploring before continuing the walk. Short narrow lanes lead up to the spacious green, lined with cottages, farms and barns, with the pub tucked away at the far end. The medieval church occupies an idyllic position on the banks of the tree-shaded River Skirfare close to the bridge.

After crossing the bridge, turn left and, passing the lych-gate of the church on the left, keep ahead through a gate at a public footpath sign for Hawkswick. Passing a large house on the right, go through a gate into a field to follow a most attractive path across meadows to Hawkswick, a distance of 1½ miles (2·25 km). Again this is an easy path to follow, the route clearly indicated by stiles, footpath signs and yellow waymarks, sometimes staying close to the river and, at other times, a few hundred yards away from it. Approaching Hawkswick, turn left over a footbridge, then right (**B**) along the opposite bank of the river. Proceed through the village and, at a public footpath sign to Kettlewell, turn left (**C**) along a track by the side of a cottage on the left, climb a stile and take the uphill path ahead. The path bears right by a wall on the right and continues climbing, roughly parallel with the valley on the right, to a gate and ladder stile. Climb over and keep ahead, still climbing steadily, to approach a wall on the right. After a while the path begins to head away from the wall, making for a footpath sign. Continue uphill to a prominent cairn, from where there are magnificent views down both Littondale and Wharfedale.

At this point turn sharp left (**D**), heading over the brow of Knipe Scar to a wall and ladder stile. Climb over and bear half-left to follow a path across rough grassland, making for the corner of the ridge in front. Soon the buildings of Kettlewell, down below in the valley, come into view. Continue along the path as it proceeds downhill, diagonally along the side of the valley, heading towards Kettlewell. Climb a ladder stile near the top edge of a wood, and continue about 50 yards (46 m) ahead to a gate in a wall next to another ladder stile. Go through the gate and along a path, which soon bears sharp left by the edge of the wood, heading steeply downhill through the trees, clearly marked by yellow signs, to the road. Here turn left for the short distance back to Kettlewell Bridge and village.

53

19 Clapham, Crummack Dale and Austwick

Start:	Clapham
Distance:	7 miles (11·25 km). Shorter version 4½ miles (7·25 km)
Approximate time:	3½ hours (2 hours for shorter version)
Parking:	Clapham
Refreshments:	Cafés and pub at Clapham, pub at Austwick
Ordnance Survey maps:	Landranger 98 (Wensleydale & Upper Wharfedale) and Outdoor Leisure 2 (Yorkshire Dales — Western area)

General description From the attractive village of Clapham, the walk starts by following one of the innumerable walled lanes in the area, before diverting to see the fascinating geological phenomena known as the Norber Erratics. With superb views all round, the route continues into the remote and almost uninhabited Crummack Dale, before proceeding along more walled lanes to the village of Austwick and returning across fields to Clapham. The walk traverses some of the finest limestone scenery.

Clapham has all the ingredients one could wish for in a Dales village: a wide main street lined by old stone cottages and houses, a stony beck running down the middle of it, crossed by several picturesque bridges, and an attractive church at the far end. Although lying beneath the bare slopes of Ingleborough, the village is surrounded by much woodland, the result of the activities of the Farrer family of Ingleborough Hall, who planted thousands of trees and remodelled the village in the nineteenth century. The best known member of this family was the botanist and writer Reginald Farrer (1880 – 1920), who introduced over 100 new plants into Europe.

Start by turning right out of the car park and walking towards the church, mostly rebuilt in the nineteenth century, apart from the tower. At the church turn right and almost immediately left in front of the entrance to Ingleborough Hall, where there is a public bridle-way sign to Austwick. Continue under two tunnels, built by the Farrers to enable people to use the bridle-way without being seen by the residents of the hall, and ahead along the broad track (**A**), an ancient pack-horse route between Richmond

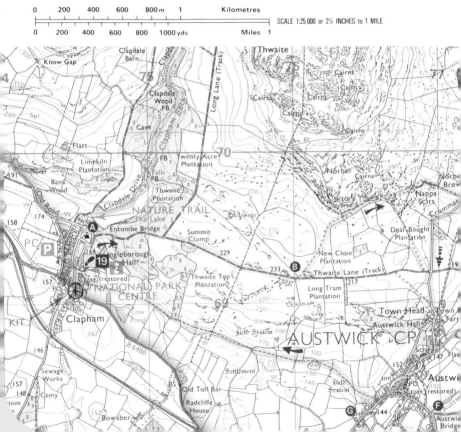

SCALE 1:25 000 or 2½ INCHES to 1 MILE

and Lancaster called Thwaite Lane. The track climbs gently past a plantation on the left and soon levels out, giving fine views over to the right. At the end of the plantation, keep straight ahead, following signs for Austwick. On the left a line of limestone scars can be seen.

After one mile (1·5 km) turn left over a ladder stile, at a public footpath sign for Norber (**B**), and head across a field, aiming for its far right-hand corner. Follow a wall as it curves to the right, climb a ladder stile and continue ahead, now immediately under the scar to the left. After about 200 yards (184 m), where the wall curves again to the right, keep ahead uphill to a signpost. Here a brief detour to the left allows you to see the Norber Erratics, a collection of boulders carried by a glacier and deposited on this plateau during the Ice Age. Because they are of ancient Silurian slate, which is harder and more resistant to erosion than limestone, these boulders have been left perched above and strewn across the landscape, sometimes on narrow pedestals as the rest of the limestone has worn away beneath them.

Return downhill to the signpost, turn left, following directions to Crummack, and keep ahead across this wild, boulder-strewn landscape, drawing towards a wall on the right. Turn right over a ladder stile and bear slightly left across a field, making for a gap in the wall in front. Pass through that gap and follow the path ahead beneath the cliffs of Nappa Scar.

A ladder stile leads the way into lonely Crummack Dale

Here there are more fine views, especially ahead looking up Crummack Dale. Keeping by a wall on the left, climb a ladder stile, cross a lane and climb another ladder stile ahead (**C**).

At this point, instead of climbing the ladder stile in front, walkers wishing to omit the Crummack Dale section can turn right and follow the lane into Austwick, rejoining the route there.

Turn left over a stile and keep ahead across a series of fields and over a succession of ladder stiles. After the third stile, proceed downhill towards the wall in front and bear right to walk parallel to that wall. Approaching the bottom corner of the field, look out for some stone steps on the left. Climb those and keep ahead for a few yards to cross a stream via a simple stone footbridge (**D**). Continue for a few yards to the end of a wall, turn right near another footbridge, and follow a winding, walled lane for ¾ mile (1 km) into the hamlet of Wharfe.

Here bear left and right, still keeping along a walled lane, to reach a tarmac lane (**E**). Turn right for about 100 yards (92 m) and, at a public bridle-way sign for Wood Lane, turn left towards a farm. Just before the farm, bear right along another walled lane and follow this for just over a mile (1·5 km) to Austwick. At a junction of walled lanes, turn left and keep ahead to a road. Turn right over the bridge (**F**) into Austwick, another attractive village and a harmonious mixture of old and new buildings.

At a road junction in the centre of the village, turn left, signposted Clapham, past the nineteenth-century church, turning right at a gate and stone stile, where there is a public footpath sign to Clapham (**G**). Soon bear left and head slightly uphill to a ladder stile. From here the route back to Clapham is an easy one, along a more or less straight path, clearly marked by a succession of stiles and, towards the end, metal gates. Finally the path passes a farm on the left, where a stile on the right leads directly into the car park.

20 Buckden and Langstrothdale Chase

Start:	Buckden
Distance:	7 miles (11·25 km)
Approximate time:	3 ½ hours
Parking:	Buckden
Refreshments:	Café and pub at Buckden, pub at Cray, pub at Hubberholme
Ordnance Survey maps:	Landranger 98 (Wensleydale & Upper Wharfedale) and Outdoor Leisure 30 (Yorkshire Dales – Northern & Central areas)

General description *This walk starts at the village of Buckden in Upper Wharfedale and the first stage is over the lower flanks of Buckden Pike to the hamlet of Cray. It continues high up along the edge of the dale, across the former hunting country of Langstrothdale Chase, to drop down to the river at the remote hamlet of Yockenthwaite. The return journey keeps by the Wharfe for most of the way, passing through the small village of Hubberholme with its interesting and beautifully situated medieval church. Two modest climbs are encountered.*

Buckden occupies a superb position above the Wharfe and its name, meaning valley of the bucks, reflects that this was once a hunting area. Go through a gate at the far end of the car park, where there is a public footpath sign to Buckden Pike and Cray High Bridge, and take the path ahead which follows the line of a Roman road from Ilkley to Bainbridge. At first it climbs through trees and rocks and later emerges into more open country, keeping by a wall on the left and still heading uphill. After the path levels off, continue by the wall, passing through two gates. There are fine views all around at this point. Soon after the second gate, the wall ends but keep straight ahead along the flat, broad, green path.

Just after climbing a stone stile by a gate, turn left through a gate, at a public footpath sign for Cray (**A**), and head downhill towards the pub at Cray which lies straight ahead. At the bottom go through a gate, cross first a stream and then the road, and turn left behind the White Lion (**B**). Bear right uphill, pass through two gates and keep ahead along a broad path. Pass through another gate, at a public footpath sign for Scar House and Yockenthwaite, and keep ahead along a most attractive path which follows the contours of the hill. Go through a gate, cross a field to another gate, go through that and keep ahead to pass through yet another gate and, proceeding slightly downhill, turn left over a stream. Continue ahead by a low wall on the left along a path which follows the edge of the dale just above the tree-line.

0	200	400	600	800m	1	Kilometres

0	200	400	600	800	1000 yds	Miles 1

SCALE 1:25 000 or 2½ INCHES to 1 MILE

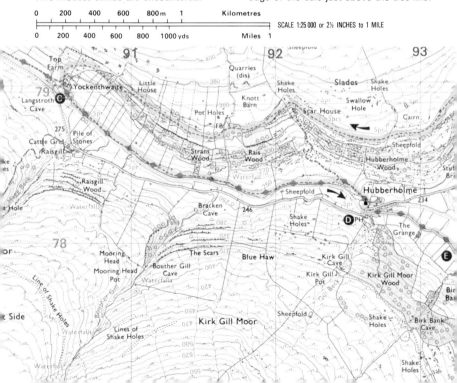

The bridge and church at Hubberholme in Upper Wharfedale

This part of the route is across the edge of Langstrothdale Chase, an ancient hunting area that, after the Norman Conquest, became the preserve of the earls of Northumberland. It was originally settled by Norse farmers, as indicated by such place names as Hubberholme and Yockenthwaite. The walking is excellent: good springy turf, limestone outcrops and magnificent views down the length of Wharfedale.

Climb a stone stile and keep ahead, dropping down towards a farmhouse below on the left and following the path to the left, around the edge of the farm buildings, to climb another stile. Keep ahead, go through a gate to enter a wood and, at the far end of the wood, climb two stone stiles and cross a footbridge. Then bear left, heading slightly downhill to climb a stone stile, following the yellow waymarks over several more stone stiles and all the while keeping along the edge

of the dale, passing limestone platforms with stumpy-looking trees growing out of them. Look out for a yellow arrow in a low wall on the left; here the path bears left and heads downhill towards the scattered hamlet of Yockenthwaite. Climb a stile, continue ahead to another stile, climb that and turn left downhill to the hamlet and river.

Approaching the river, turn left along a track, at a public footpath sign for Hubberholme **(C)**, follow the track through a gate and across a small field to a stile. Climb over and immediately bear right to a gap in the wall and go down some steps. For the next 1½ miles (2·25 km) follow the riverside path; a very pleasant, well waymarked route across meadows and through several gates and over stiles. When the squat tower of Hubberholme church comes into sight, keep by the wall on the right and turn right along a track to the bridge.

The thirteenth-century church, in a serene setting by the river, backed by the wooded hills of the chase, looks a typical small village church from the outside but the interior has several interesting features. For a start, the walls and columns are of rough stonework which give it an unusually rugged appearance. The church also possesses a rare sixteenth-century rood-loft, which used to support a rood or crucifix. The pews are a more recent feature, made by the 'mouse-man', Robert Thompson of Kilburn, who leaves carvings of small mice as his hallmark. Over the eighteenth-century bridge is the George Inn, originally the vicarage and remaining church property until as recently as 1965.

Cross the bridge and turn left **(D)** along the lane in front of the inn. With a good view of Buckden Pike in front, keep along the lane as far as a large gate on the left, where there is a public footpath sign to Buckden Bridge **(E)**. Pass through, walk along the edge of a field with a wall on the left, soon rejoining the river-bank, and keep by the river up to Buckden Bridge. Turn left and follow the road back into Buckden village.

21 Giggleswick Scar and Stainforth Force

Start:	Settle
Distance:	8 miles (12·75 km)
Approximate time:	4 hours
Parking:	Settle
Refreshments:	Plenty of pubs, cafés and restaurants in Settle
Ordnance Survey maps:	Landranger 98 (Wensleydale & Upper Wharfedale) and Outdoor Leisure 2 (Yorkshire Dales – Western area)

General description From the busy market town of Settle, the route first climbs up onto Giggleswick Scar, from where there are extensive views. It then cuts across wild and open country, via the secluded hamlet of Feizor, for a spectacular drop into Ribblesdale at Little Stainforth. The final stretch is a delightful ramble along the banks of the Ribble, passing a picturesque pack-horse bridge and, just below it, the impressive Stainforth Force. There are three separate climbs but none of them steep or strenuous.

Like most of the larger market towns of the Yorkshire Dales, Settle lies on a river, astride a main road, at the point where the narrow uplands of the dale broaden out into a wider and greener valley. Downstream from Settle the Ribble flows more serenely and, unlike most Dales rivers, turns west to the Irish Sea instead of eastwards to the Humber and North Sea. The town has an attractive market square, narrow winding streets that lead into small squares and, with plenty of gift shops, inns and cafés, makes an excellent walking centre.

Start by walking northwards along the A65, over the river and into Giggleswick, a small village with a fifteenth-century church and noted for its public school, whose green-domed chapel makes a distinctive landmark. Where the road bends sharply to the right, turn right along a side road called The Mains (A) and follow it uphill past houses. At the end of the road, continue along a track, soon joining another track coming in from the right, and climb through woodland, bearing gradually to the left.

Leaving the trees, pass through a gate into more open country, bear right by a stone wall and continue uphill, keeping by the wall on the right. The path, not very clear on the ground but well waymarked, now squeezes between the edge of a quarry on the left and

a stone wall on the right and continues across the flanks of Giggleswick Scar. At this point there are superb views all around, over Ribblesdale to the east, the Bowland Fells to the west, Settle behind and, in the distance, the distinctive outline of Pendle Hill, associated with the Lancashire witches. Bear left towards a cairn and, just before reaching it, turn right along the green path which follows the edge of the scar above the main road.

This is a good spot to observe how the scar was formed. It is part of the Craven Fault, a fracture caused by massive earth movements which lifted the rocks high above the surrounding countryside on one side but caused them to slip down on the other. The main road follows the line of the fault.

Keep ahead just below the ridge all the while, going over a ladder stile and drawing gradually closer to the road. Climb another ladder stile, continue ahead, bearing slightly right, away from the wall on the left, up through a gate at a public footpath sign and bear half-right across the grass (B), uphill to another gate. Pass through that and keep straight ahead along a grassy path; now there are more fine views ahead, including Pen-y-ghent.

SCALE 1:25 000 or 2½ INCHES to 1 MILE

58

barn to another gate. Pass through that, bear right and continue by a wall on the right. Where the walls converge, turn right through a gate, bear left across a field, first keeping by a wall on the left and then heading right away from it, to a ladder stile in the top right-hand corner of the field. Climb that, turn left and take the path which proceeds through a pass between hills on either side. Go through a gap in a wall, keep ahead and, shortly after meeting a wall on the right, climb a stone stile and continue to a gap in another wall. Pass through that, keep ahead towards another wall, climb a ladder stile and turn right at a public footpath sign to Stainforth. Continue slightly uphill, following a green path and heading away from the wall on the right, and over the brow, where there is a dramatic view over Ribblesdale.

Climb a ladder stile and keep ahead in a straight line to start dropping into the valley. Heading towards farm buildings in front, climb another ladder stile to pick up a track which drops down to a gate. Go through that and keep ahead along a tarmac lane into Little Stainforth. Continue straight ahead at the road junction down to the river.

Just before the old pack-horse bridge, built in 1670 to link Stainforth with Little Stainforth, turn right along a very attractive riverside path (D), reaching Stainforth Force in a few yards. Here the Ribble cascades over a series of ledges, a most impressive sight when in full spate. Continue along the riverbank, over a ladder stile and ahead. The path continues high above a wooded stretch of the river, over a ladder stile and down steps to rejoin the river-bank. The rest of the way to Stackhouse keeps by or above the river, passing over several stiles.

After climbing a stone stile by the weir and footbridge at Stackhouse (E), turn right along a walled track into the hamlet. Turn left at a tarmac lane and, at a public footpath sign (F), turn left through a gap in the wall and walk across the middle of a field towards a stile in the wall ahead. Climb it, continue along the path to rejoin the river, climb two stiles and head straight across a large field to another stile. Climb that and proceed around the edge of a playing field up to the main road and bridge. Here turn left, back into Settle.

The Ribble surges under the pack-horse bridge and over Stainforth Force

Climb a ladder stile and continue ahead, drawing close to a wall on the left and climbing another ladder stile. Keep ahead along another grassy path, which proceeds gently downhill, joining a wall on the right and following it as it curves down towards the hamlet of Feizor. Go through a gate, turn right and walk along the lane through the hamlet.

Where the lane bends left, bear right (C) along a track between buildings, go through a gate by a barn and around the edge of the

22 Bolton Abbey, Barden Tower and The Strid

Start:	Bolton Abbey
Distance:	8 miles (12·75 km)
Approximate time:	4 hours
Parking:	Bolton Abbey
Refreshments:	Café at Bolton Abbey, restaurant at Barden Tower and the Cavendish Pavilion café between The Strid and Bolton Abbey
Ordnance Survey maps:	Landranger 104 (Leeds, Bradford & Harrogate) and Outdoor Leisure 10 (Yorkshire Dales – Southern area)

General description *It is no wonder that Bolton Abbey has inspired both famous artists, including Turner, and not so famous ones, and is such a popular subject for calendars. The ruins harmonise perfectly with their exquisite setting, where meadow, moorland, woodland and the great sweep of the Wharfe create a scene of unrivalled beauty. A short distance upstream is The Strid, where the Wharfe narrows to a mere stream and plunges through a spectacular, rocky, tree-lined gorge. Still further upstream it flows below the substantial ruins of Barden Tower. All these features are combined in this splendid and sometimes dramatic walk. There is a lengthy but gradual climb at the beginning and some narrow rocky paths by The Strid but otherwise the route presents no problems.*

From the car park turn left along the road to Burnsall and, soon after passing under an eighteenth-century arch that was once an aqueduct, bear left onto a track signposted to Halton East **(A)**. The first part of the walk, across fields, woods and moor, is easy to follow, waymarked with blue signs all the way. Pass through a gate and head across a field to a footpath sign near a wire fence and by the side of a pond. Follow the fence, go through a gate and turn right across a field to enter a wood. In a short while take a sharp left-hand turn, following blue arrows, and continue through the wood to a gate in a wall. Go through to emerge into open country, following a line of blue stones across two large fields. There are glorious views to the right up Wharfedale.

Continue through a gate and along a path parallel to a wall on the left. The path skirts Middle Hare Head on the right and goes over the shoulder of the hill, bearing slightly right to a gate. Pass through and keep ahead to the road **(B)**. Turn right and follow the road downhill for 1¼ miles (2 km) to a T-junction, turning left here **(C)** to the remains of Barden Tower.

Barden Tower belonged to the Clifford family of nearby Skipton Castle, and was originally built in the twelfth century as one of a number of hunting lodges in the Forest of Barden. The remains that we see today mostly date from the fifteenth century, when the lodge was rebuilt and extended by the tenth Lord Clifford, the 'Shepherd Lord', who preferred the rural simplicity of Barden to his main residence at Skipton. Separate from the main block is the former chapel and priest's house, the only part not ruined, and now used as a restaurant.

From the tower continue along the road down towards Barden Bridge and, just before the bridge, go through a gap in the wall on the right **(D)** and down some steps to join the riverside path. Now comes a superb three-mile (4·75 km) walk, through woods and across meadows, along or close to the banks of the Wharfe to Bolton Abbey. Soon after passing a turreted bridge, which is a Victorian aqueduct carrying water from reservoirs in Nidderdale to Bradford, cross meadows to a gate which gives access to the Strid Woods. These are owned by the Devonshire Estates and a small charge is made to walk through them. There are a number of paths through the woods, trails laid out by the Devonshire Estates, but this route follows the path closest to the river. Take care – during wet

SCALE 1:25 000 or 2½ INCHES to 1 MILE

BOLTON ABBEY CP

conditions it can become slippery and quite dangerous. Eventually The Strid is reached, heralded by the noise of the river which, at this point, is only a few yards wide and surges over the rocks as it squeezes through the narrow gorge. It is a most impressive and beautiful spot and one in which to linger but, sadly, people have lost their lives here, foolishly trying to stride (Strid) across the narrow channel.

Now the path becomes much easier, broadening out into a flat and clearly defined track which keeps ahead to a junction of tracks. Here bear slightly to the right along the wider path which climbs and then descends to the Cavendish Pavilion café and a footbridge (E). Cross the bridge, turn right along the other side of the river, climb a stile and turn left by a stream. Go across a minor road, cross a footbridge over the stream and, keeping along the road uphill for a few yards, bear right along a path signposted to Bolton Priory (F). This path winds through the woods above the river, giving splendid views of the great bend in the Wharfe and the priory ruins on the opposite bank, eventually dropping down to a footbridge. Cross over and walk up to the ruins.

Bolton was founded as a priory of Augustinian canons in 1154 but, after its dissolution in 1539, the adjoining village and local parish became known as Bolton Abbey and this is

the name which has survived. The east end of the church, rebuilt after a Scottish raid in the fourteenth century, is ruined and is dominated by the great east window which offers views of the hills beyond. In contrast, the nave of the church survived intact, as this part was always used as the local parish church and still serves that purpose today. It is unusual in that it has two west fronts: the original thirteenth-century one and an unfinished sixteenth-century one. The latter was only started twenty years before the priory was dissolved, hence its uncompleted state. The cloisters and surrounding domestic buildings have almost entirely disappeared, apart from the fourteenth-century gatehouse, incorporated in the present, mainly Victorian, Bolton Hall.

23 Pateley Bridge and Brimham Rocks

Start:	Pateley Bridge
Distance:	9 miles (14·25 km)
Approximate time:	5 hours
Parking:	Car park by the bridge in Pateley Bridge
Refreshments:	Cafés and pubs in Pateley Bridge
Ordnance Survey maps:	Landranger 99 (Northallerton & Ripon), Pathfinder SE 06/16 652 (Grassington & Pateley Bridge) and SE 26/36 653 (Fountains Abbey & Boroughbridge)

General description The incredibly weird shapes of Brimham Rocks, occupying a commanding position above Nidderdale, are the focal point of this exhilarating walk. Starting from the market town of Pateley Bridge, the outward route contours along the northern side of the dale, involving several short climbs and giving extensive views. After descending from the rocks into the valley, the return route follows the banks of the River Nidd.

Quarrying, textiles and lead-mining have all played a part in the history of Pateley Bridge but now this pleasant Nidderdale market town relies mainly on traditional agriculture and the newer and ever-growing tourist industry. From the car park by the river turn right up High Street and, where the main road bends right, carry on up Old Church Lane. Keep ahead, climbing steeply, and turn right into the churchyard of the old ruined church (**A**). A new church was built in 1827 on a different site and its medieval predecessor here was abandoned and left to decay. Like many ruins it has an attractive, melancholic atmosphere, enhanced by its scenic location high above the town and dale.

Just past the church, a gate in the wall leads into a field. Go through and follow a path straight across two fields, making for the corner of a wall in front and, shortly afterwards, a stile. Climb over, turn left along a narrow lane and, where the lane bends right, keep straight ahead along a track, at a Nidderdale Way signpost, bearing right at a path junction down to a road. Turn left, follow the road uphill for about 200 yards (184 m) and, at another Nidderdale Way sign, bear right along a wide track (**B**).

For the rest of the way to Brimham Rocks there are superb views over Nidderdale. Turn right at a tarmac lane and, after 100 yards

SCALE 1:25 000 or 2½ INCHES to 1 MILE

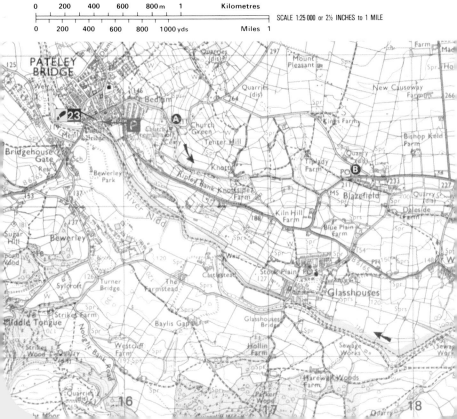

(92 m), left at a public footpath sign for Wilsill. Go through a gate, keep ahead a few yards to another gate on the left, go through that and continue across a small field to another gate. Pass through and head straight across the next field towards a complex of farm buildings. Negotiate a gate, stone stile and another gate in the far corner of that field, and keep ahead by a wall on the right. Brimham Rocks can now be seen in front, standing out boldly on the ridge. At a farm, go through two gates onto a lane, cross over and continue up the stone steps opposite to follow a narrow path between houses. Climb a stile and keep ahead across several fields, keeping by a wall on the right. Approaching farm buildings, pass through a gate, head across to a stone stile by another gate, climb that and continue along the edge of a field by a wall on the left. Pass through several more gates, turn left along a farm track for a few yards and, at the gate to the farm, bear left along a narrow walled path. Follow this path up to the next group of farm buildings and, at a junction of several paths, keep straight ahead, passing a house on the left, along a broad track.

At the next farm, turn right along a narrow path **(C)** at a Nidderdale Way sign, climb two stiles in quick succession and continue downhill across the middle of a narrow field. Now there are clear views in front of Brimham Rocks as they get closer. Pass through a narrow gap in a wall at the bottom end of the field, keep ahead by a wall on the left and

bear left through a gap in that wall down to a farm track. Here turn left and then right, at a Nidderdale Way sign, down a walled track, over a stile and bear left across a footbridge. Climb a stile and continue ahead, gradually ascending and bearing right by a wire fence on the left. Keep ahead along the left-hand edge of several fields, climbing steadily all the while. Climb another ladder stile and continue towards a farm, bearing right to a stile. Climb that and turn right, keeping the farmhouse on the left, and walk along the farm track, bearing left through an area of woodland. About 100 yards (92 m) before the track turns left to meet a road, turn right at a National Trust sign **(D)** and take the path that winds through heather and across rough grass up to the ridge on which the rocks stand.

There are a number of paths that crisscross the heathery moorland through the complex of rocks and it does not matter which you take; the views all around from this elevated position are magnificent. Brimham Rocks comprise a series of millstone grit boulders, standing twenty feet or more above the rock platform, fashioned into the most grotesque and fantastic shapes by thousands of years of weathering. In some cases they stand on slim stems of rock, like delicate wine glasses, looking as if they could topple over any minute. The nicknames given to them by some of the early Victorian tourists have remained – the Dancing Bear, the Anvil, the Sphinx, etc.

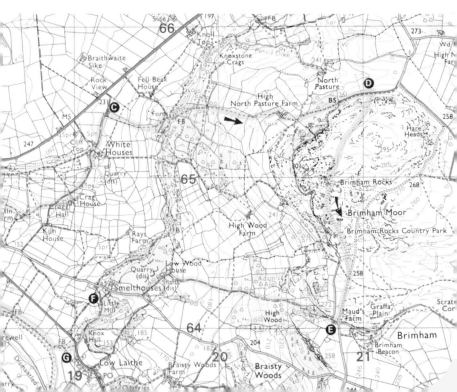

Take your time to enjoy both the rocks themselves and the surrounding views. The whole area is now owned and maintained by the National Trust and there is a shop and information centre. Whichever paths you explore through this jumble of rocks, make your way down to the large car park and walk ahead along the road to start the return journey to Pateley Bridge. At a T-junction, turn right along the road for ¼ mile (0·4 km) and, at a public bridle-way sign for Smelthouses (**E**), turn right to the right-hand one of two gates ahead, go through and follow a grassy path immediately below a low cliff. This is a most attractive path which winds downhill, through woodland and across fields, with lovely views ahead looking up Nidderdale. Approaching Smelthouses, go through a gate and turn left down a tarmac track to a road. Turn right and, where the road drops down into a small valley, turn left at a public bridle-way sign (**F**) to follow a track past houses and cottages and by a stream on the right down to another road. Go straight across, through a gap in the fence opposite, at a public footpath sign to Glasshouses, and continue ahead by a stream on the right. Climb a stone stile, shortly afterwards turn right over a footbridge and left along the opposite bank of the stream, reaching the river-bank a few yards ahead (**G**).

Here turn right to follow a delightful path by the Nidd up to Glasshouses. At Glasshouses bear right, away from the river, and then left to a road, passing fine old mill buildings on the left. At the road bear left and almost immediately right, at a public footpath sign, along a broad track by a reservoir. In a while you rejoin the river and keep by it, along a well constructed path, all the way to Pateley Bridge, a distance of about 1 ½ miles (2·25 km).

Just a few of the fantastically shaped Brimham Rocks

24 Jervaulx Abbey and Middleham

Start:	Jervaulx Abbey
Distance:	9 miles (14·25 km)
Approximate time:	5 hours
Parking:	Opposite entrance to Jervaulx Abbey
Refreshments:	Pubs and cafés in Middleham, Cover Inn between Middleham and East Witton
Ordnance Survey maps:	Landranger 99 (Northallerton & Ripon) and First Series SE 18 (Middleham)

General description *Many of the Yorkshire Dales have an abbey and castle reasonably close to each other and which can be linked by attractive footpaths, thus providing historic focal points amidst fine scenery. Wensleydale is no exception and this lovely walk through the wide, green and more gentle lower part of the dale links the rather grim, stark ruins of Middleham Castle with the beautifully situated, tranquil, mellowed stones of Jervaulx Abbey. Although a reasonably lengthy walk, there are only two climbs, both of which are short and easy.*

Turn right out of the car park along the road and, after ¼ mile (0·4 km), take the lane on the right, signposted Ellingstring and Healey (**A**). Follow it uphill for ¾ mile (1 km) and, where it levels off, turn right along the track to Hammer Farm (**B**). This track keeps along the lower slopes of Witton Fell on the left and gives expansive views across Wensleydale to the right.

Keeping to the left of the house, go through the farmyard and bear right through a gate and across a field. There is no clear path, but head in the direction of East Witton Church in front and, after passing through a gate by a wall, continue ahead to pick up a distinct path which heads downhill, through another gate and along the edge of a small ravine on the left. Go through a gate in front, over a stream and along a track which descends past farms and cottages into East Witton (**C**). In the village, turn left along the side of the uncommonly long (¼ mile (0·4 km)) and wide green, lined both sides by stone cottages.

At the end of the green, keep along a lane for a few yards and turn right through the first gate into a field. The next section of the route is, fortunately, well waymarked with arrows; very convenient as the paths are not always clear and the route is somewhat tortuous. On entering the field, immediately turn left and head across it towards a barn, pass through a gate beside it and continue across the next field. Climb a stile ahead, cross the next field to another stile and climb that to join a winding track. Where that track ends at a field gate in front, go through a gate on the left and along a grassy path by the side of a plantation. Turn left at the next gate, keep along the edge of a field and, where the plantation ends, continue by a wall on the left.

Pass through another gate, continue across the next field and, about half-way across, turn left through a gate and immediately right, keeping ahead by a wall on the right. Go through yet another gate, continue by the left-hand side of a hedge and, at a wall corner, keep ahead across the middle of the field. Just before the far end of it, bear right through a gate and turn left, keeping by a hedge and fence on the left. At the end of the field, climb a fence, cross a stream and carry on across the next field, heading towards the wooded banks of the River Cover and the far right-hand corner. Here pass through a gate and keep ahead, parallel to the river below, joining a wire fence on the left. When Hullo Bridge comes into sight, bear right towards it, cross over (**D**) and continue uphill, by a wall on the right, across the open expanses of Middleham Moor. At this stage do not be

Middleham Castle – grim walls in an attractive setting

surprised by the sound of hoofs and the sight of horses; this area is renowned for racehorse training. At the road, turn right along the wide verge by the side of it into Middleham and up to the castle, whose forbidding walls dominate the small grey stone town.

Middleham Castle has a basically simple design, with a huge twelfth-century Norman keep, 105 ft by 78 ft with walls 10 to 12 ft thick, surrounded by a thirteenth-century curtain wall, with a gatehouse in the south-east corner. For two centuries it was one of the strongholds of the powerful Nevilles, the earls of Warwick, but after the death of Richard Neville (Warwick the Kingmaker) at the battle of Barnet in 1471, it was forfeited to the Crown. Edward IV gave it to his brother, Richard of Gloucester (later Richard III), and it became his principal residence until

his seizure of the throne in 1483. Middleham is a pleasant little town – only the size of a village but with the appearance of a town – with two squares, a medieval church and a number of imposing Georgian houses and inns. The inns and cafés around the main square make an excellent excuse for a break at just over the half-way stage.

From the centre of Middleham the route continues for ½ mile (0·8 km) along the road to Ripon, before bearing right (E) along a straight broad track, which later becomes a narrow path ending at a metal gate. Pass through this gate and keep ahead along the edge of a field down to the River Cover (F), turning left to follow the river-bank up to the road. Turn right over the bridge, by the Cover Inn, and immediately left along the other bank of the river (G). Soon you reach the

SCALE 1:25 000 or 2½ INCHES to 1 MILE

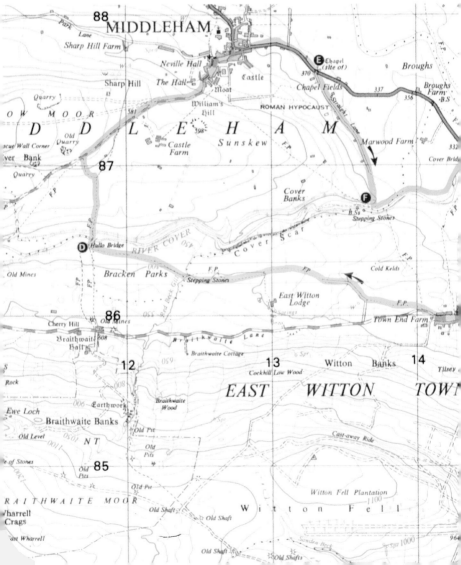

confluence of the Cover and Ure and the rest of the walk (about 1½ miles or 2·25 km) is a pleasant and relaxing ramble along the broad grassy banks of the Ure, with wide views across fields all the way. On approaching Jervaulx Hall the path bends right, through a gate and up to the road. Turn left past Jervaulx Hall and keep along the road to the entrance to the abbey, opposite the car park.

Like most of the monasteries of the Yorkshire Dales, Jervaulx grew rich from the proceeds of sheep-farming, but in addition its monks made cheese and bred horses, thereby creating two of the principal activities of this part of Wensleydale. Compared with some of its neighbours, its ruins, especially those of the church, are fragmentary, but it compensates for this with its superb parkland location and wonderfully tranquil atmos-

phere. It seems to have had a generally tranquil history too, for apart from the execution of its last abbot, Adam of Sedbergh, for trying to resist closure in 1536, nothing eventful seems to have happened here either during the Middle Ages or subsequently.

The most substantial surviving portions are the chapter house, with three fine Norman arches, the kitchen, the monk's dormitory and the infirmary. One of the most appealing aspects of Jervaulx is the apparently random jumble of ruined walls, pillars and stones, with climbing plants all over and an absence of neatly trimmed lawns and information boards, making the ruins seem more authentic and satisfying. On a fine day it is an excellent spot in which to linger and relax at the end of the walk.

25 Garsdale Head and Hellgill

Start:	Garsdale Head, just below Garsdale Station
Distance:	8 miles (12·75 km)
Approximate time:	4½ hours
Parking:	Park by side of road near Garsdale Station
Refreshments:	None
Ordnance Survey maps:	Landranger 98 (Wensleydale & Upper Wharfedale) and Pathfinder SD 69/79 617 (Sedbergh & Baugh Fell)

General description *Much of this walk is across the bleak and open moorlands around Garsdale and Upper Wensleydale, in one of the less frequented parts of the Yorkshire Dales, and the starkness, loneliness and austerity of the scenery is both appealing and exhilarating. This is very much a 'fine weather' walk; with no visible footpaths and a lack of clearly identifiable landmarks in some parts it is not recommended except in clear conditions.*

Garsdale is a long narrow dale, bounded by Baugh Fell on the north and Rise Hill on the south, linking Hawes and Sedbergh. It contains no villages; just a scattering of farms and cottages. From below the station at Garsdale Head, walk down to the road, cross over, climb a stone stile and go through a gate, at a public footpath sign for Grisedale and Flust. Keeping ahead by a wall on the left, bear slightly right to go through a gate and continue parallel with the wall. Immediately you are surrounded by a landscape of wild, bleak, open fells. Soon drop down to join a stream on the left for a few yards and then turn right, climbing steeply. At the top of the ridge, bear left to follow a path along to a stile, a gate and a footpath sign. Go through and keep ahead in the direction of the sign, soon passing a farm on the left. Just past the farm, turn left over a stone stile in a wall and bear right, at first continuing parallel to the wall but later bearing slightly away from it over another stone stile. Walk across the middle of the next field, bearing slightly left over a stone stile, and keep ahead towards a farm. Cross a stream and, keeping to the left of the farm, climb a stone stile; continue straight ahead to climb another stile just past a farm, and carry on to join a road near the farmhouse in front **(A)**.

Keep ahead along this road as it winds up Grisedale to the next farm. Continue past the farm to a gate, go through and follow a track as it turns sharp right. Shortly afterwards it meets another track. Here turn right along it for a few yards and then bear left **(B)**, in a north-easterly direction, across the feature-less expanses of Grisedale Common. There is no visible footpath but keep in a straight line across the rough moorland and, on reaching the brow of the hill, look out for a gate by the corner of a wall. Go through that and keep ahead by a wall on the right to start descending into Upper Wensleydale. Where the wall starts to bend to the right, keep ahead (again no visible footpath), gradually bearing left across more rough moorland and eventually walking parallel with the valley below. Keep above the valley and, on seeing a farm in front, head straight towards it. Pass through a gate and continue ahead, passing the ruined farm building on the left, through a metal gate, over a stream by a waterfall and ahead by a wall on the right. Now keep by that wall in a fairly straight line, parallel to the road and the Settle – Carlisle railway line on the right, for a mile (1·5 km). Approaching a farm, go through a gate, keep ahead to rejoin the wall, pass through another gate and continue by a wire fence, turning right at a metal gate down to the road **(C)**.

Cross over, and at a public footpath sign to Elmgill and Hellgill, turn right by Aisgill Moor cottages and cross the railway line at Aisgill Summit, the highest point on the Settle – Carlisle line. Now follow a broad track round to the left and up to Hellgill Force, a waterfall on the infant River Eden. From here there is a striking view northwards over the bare flanks of Mallerstang Common to Wild Boar Fell. The track turns sharp right just before the river and soon bears left across a footbridge, then right, along the other side of the river. Follow the track past a farm on the left and, keeping ahead by a wall on the left, pass through a gate and turn right, immediately through another gate, to Hell Gill Bridge **(D)**.

Cross the bridge, keep ahead along a grassy track for about 200 yards (184 m) and then bear left, along a narrower and fainter grassy path, towards a ruined farm below a group of trees in front. At this point you are crossing the watershed between streams that feed the rivers Eden and Ure. The Eden, unique for a Dales river, flows northwards from here to the Solway Firth while the Ure flows southwards through Wensleydale. You are also following an ancient routeway called the High Way.

In a while pick up a wall on the right, cross the infant Ure and keep ahead to go through a ford. Bear right towards a farm, and, just before the ruined building, turn right through two gates and bear left across grassland (no definite path) in the direction of a plantation, clearly seen ahead on the opposite slopes of

Wild Boar Fell from Hellgill Force

the valley. Follow a more or less straight route through a gap in a wall, over two stone stiles, through a gate and another gap by a barn, through another gate, over a stone stile, through one more gate and finally ahead, by a wall on the right, to a gate near a farm. Go through, across a farm track and through another gate, keeping ahead to a footbridge and stile (E). Turn right, by the side of the small, plain eighteenth-century Lunds Chapel, to a gate and continue across the River Ure along a track into a plantation.

Where the track starts to bear right, keep ahead at a public footpath sign, climb a stile and continue along a rough path through the trees. Emerging from the plantation, bear right a few yards to a stile, climb over, immediately over another stone stile opposite and ahead across a field, making for a third stone stile in the wall on the right. Climb that, cross the next field to another stone stile by a gate, climb over and continue straight ahead to another stile, by a public footpath sign, to join a road (F). Turn left along the road for ¼ mile (0·4 km) and, about 100 yards (92 m) before a phone box, turn right (G) at a public

footpath sign for East Mud Becks, over a stile and through a gate, heading towards a footbridge over the railway line.

Cross the bridge, pass through a gate in the wall by the railway line, walk down some steps and turn half-right (H) to head in a straight line, once more across bare and featureless moorland with no discernible path. A stone stile in a wall indicates the right direction; climb that and keep ahead uphill. Over to the left is the Dandrymire Viaduct, one of a number of similarly impressive structures on the Settle – Carlisle railway. Look out for a stile in the next wall that lies ahead over the brow of the hill, climb that and keep ahead, now picking up a definite path, to a stone stile in the next wall. Climb over and continue, downhill and slightly up again, to another stone stile in a wall. Climb that and continue down towards the road. Again it is difficult to see a path but keep towards the right of the farm buildings ahead to a stone stile and public footpath sign. Turn right along the road and first left to Garsdale Station.

26 Gunnerside, Kisdon and Muker

Start:	Gunnerside
Distance:	10½ miles (16·5 km) (Muker and Kisdon section only, 5½ miles (8·75 km))
Approximate time:	5½ hours (3 hours for Muker and Kisdon only)
Parking:	Parking area in centre of Gunnerside
Refreshments:	Café and pub at Gunnerside, cafés and pub at Muker
Ordnance Survey maps:	Landranger 92 (Barnard Castle) and 98 (Wensleydale & Upper Wharfedale), Outdoor Leisure 30 (Yorkshire Dales – Northern & Central areas)

General description *Most of this walk is either along, or just above, the banks of the River Swale and traverses some of the most majestic riverside scenery in the Dales. It is a walk of magnificent vistas, at high and low levels, and tremendous variety: riverside meadows, hills, woods, waterfalls, two attractive villages and, at one point, a*

dramatic viewpoint down the length of Swaledale.

In the nineteenth century, Gunnerside was a lead-mining community and Gunnerside Gill, to the north, still bears the scars and ruins of the lead-mining industry. Nowadays, however, the village has all the usual appealing qualities of a rural Dales settlement: attractive stone cottages, pleasant village square, pub and tea-rooms and a fine position amidst meadows that sweep down to the river.

Facing south in the direction of the river, turn right past cottages, go through a gate with a yellow arrow and footpath sign to Ivelet and Muker, and walk along a paved path, through a new housing development, to a gate at the far end. Pass through, cross a field towards a stone stile, climb over and follow a grassy path across several fields and through a number of stone stiles and gates in a straight line, following the side of the valley with the river below. Approaching the steep-sided river-bank, bear right at a footpath sign by a wire fence on the left, continue through a gate and along the edge of the cliff above the Swale, now with a wire fence on the right. Head across several more fields and over stone stiles, still keeping in a straight line and, soon after dropping down to a foot-bridge over a stream, enter the hamlet of Ivelet (**A**). Turn left at a lane and follow it down to the riverside.

A glorious panorama down Swaledale above Muker

At the picturesque Ivelet Bridge, keep ahead through a gate, at a public footpath sign to Muker **(B)**, and along the riverside path. The next section of the route is easy to follow as, for the most part, it keeps by the Swale and is clearly waymarked. It is a particularly lovely stretch of riverside walking. Keep by the sparkling river for just over a mile (1·5 km) and, on seeing the houses of Muker ahead, bear right and head in a straight line across more fields and over stone stiles, cutting off a corner where the river bends to the right. On rejoining the river, bear right, once more keeping along its bank. Ignoring the footbridge on the left **(C)**, keep ahead for the next 2½ miles (4 km) along the side of the increasingly steep, wooded dale opposite the bulk of Kisdon Hill on the other side of the river. After dropping down to a footbridge by a waterfall at Swinner Gill, the path climbs steeply above the edge of the valley, giving magnificent views. Continue along it as it starts to drop down towards Keld and, after crossing a footbridge, turn left off the main path, drop down to another footbridge and cross over, pausing to admire the impressive fall, one of several in this part of Swaledale.

Bear right through a gate, walk up a steep path and, at the top, turn sharp left at a Pennine Way sign **(D)**. Go through a gate and keep ahead, with superb views through the trees of the river below, continuing beneath a steep cliff on the right. At a public footpath sign, bear right, following Pennine Way signs, and follow a clear, well way-

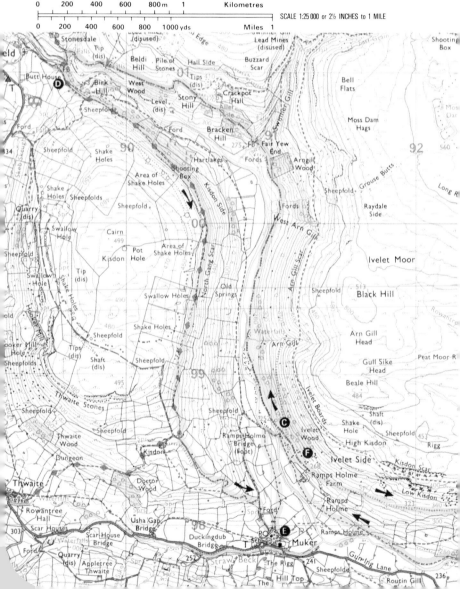

SCALE 1:25 000 or 2½ INCHES to 1 MILE

marked path along the valley, high above riverside woods. The path twists and turns over the shoulder of Kisdon Hill giving superb views, especially just before the descent to Muker where there is a spectacular vista down Swaledale, surely one of the finest in the Dales. At a T-junction of paths, bear left along a walled track and follow it as it zig-zags downhill into Muker.

Muker is the most idyllic of Swaledale villages and the cluster of cottages, church, pub and, unusual for this area, the classical style Literary Institute, above the beck make a most memorable sight. Entering the village, first bear left and then turn sharp left (E), at a public footpath sign to Gunnerside and Keld, climbing a stone stile and proceeding along a path, across a succession of small fields and over a series of stone stiles, back down to the Swale. At the river, turn sharp right, cross

the footbridge and turn right again at a public footpath sign for Gunnerside. After following part of the outward route for a short while, bear left at a public footpath sign to Gunnerside via Road (F), along an uphill path which joins a broad track.

Here bear right and, in a short while, this track becomes a narrow tarmac lane which you keep along for 2½ miles (4 km) back to Gunnerside. The lane climbs high above the dale and, not surprisingly, the views from it all the way are magnificent, making an excellent conclusion to a long but extremely scenic and absorbing walk.

A shorter version of this walk is to start at Muker (E), follow directions to the River Swale at (C) and do the middle section of the walk along the river to (D) and back over the shoulder of Kisdon Hill to Muker.

27 Pen-y-ghent

Start:	Horton in Ribblesdale
Distance:	6 miles (9·5 km)
Approximate time:	3½ hours
Parking:	Horton in Ribblesdale
Refreshments:	Café and pubs at Horton in Ribblesdale
Ordnance Survey maps:	Landranger 98 (Wensleydale & Upper Wharfedale), Outdoor Leisure 2 (Yorkshire Dales – Western area)

General description *Pen-y-ghent, one of the famed 'Three Peaks' of Yorkshire, is a mecca for keen hill walkers, its distinctive whaleback shape dominating Ribblesdale and the surrounding area for miles. The ascent is steep in parts with some scrambling but is not difficult; the descent is both gradual and without problems. The final section is along one of the numerous Pennine 'walled lanes'*

but, before that, a short detour enables you to see a dramatic pot-hole.

The walk starts in the farming and quarrying village of Horton in Ribblesdale. From the car park, walk along the main road towards the solid-looking, greystone Norman church, from where there is a dramatic view of the chief objective of the walk. Just past the church, cross a stream and turn left along a narrow lane, with the stream on the left **(A)**. After a while the lane bends right, away from the stream, and towards Brackenbottom.

Just before reaching the hamlet, turn left, at a public footpath sign for Pen-y-ghent **(B)**, go past a barn, climb a stile and then bear left along the side of a wall on the left. Now a steady ascent begins and, as you climb, the views over the surrounding countryside become ever more extensive and superb. Climb a ladder stile and keep ahead, climbing all the while and encountering rougher terrain, with a little bit of scrambling over rocks here and there. Over to the right are the smooth bare flanks of Fountains Fell. Climb

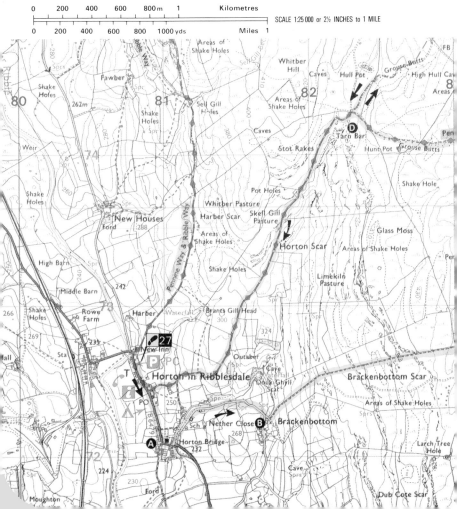

The church at Horton in Ribblesdale with Pen-y-ghent behind it

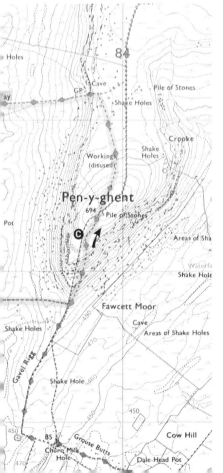

another ladder stile, continue up a stepped path to a third stile, climb that, turn left and now start to climb much more steeply. Follow the path that skirts the right-hand edge of some crags and keep ahead towards the top. The route is now very steep and rocky but is marked by cairns and, after some further scrambling, continue by a wall on the left to reach the 2,277 ft- (694 m-) high summit (**C**).

As might be expected from such a height, the all-round views are magnificent, especially across Ribblesdale to the sister peaks of Ingleborough and Whernside. At the summit, turn left over a ladder stile and proceed downhill along a stony path. Keep ahead until the path bears right near the edge of a steep cliff and follow a clear, broad path downhill along the edge of the cliff, turning sharp left at a public footpath sign for Horton. Continue across bleak open moorland and, near the bottom, climb a ladder stile, keep ahead to another ladder stile by a gate, climb that and a few yards ahead is a T-junction of paths (**D**).

Here turn right to make a short detour to view Hull Pot. Its deep chasm with sheer sides is a most impressive sight, especially after rain, when water thunders over the side and down into the cave. Retracing your steps from the pot, continue ahead through a gate and along Horton Scar Lane, a walled track that leads back to Horton in Ribblesdale. Approaching the village, bear right at a junction of tracks, continue down to the main road and turn right back to the car park.

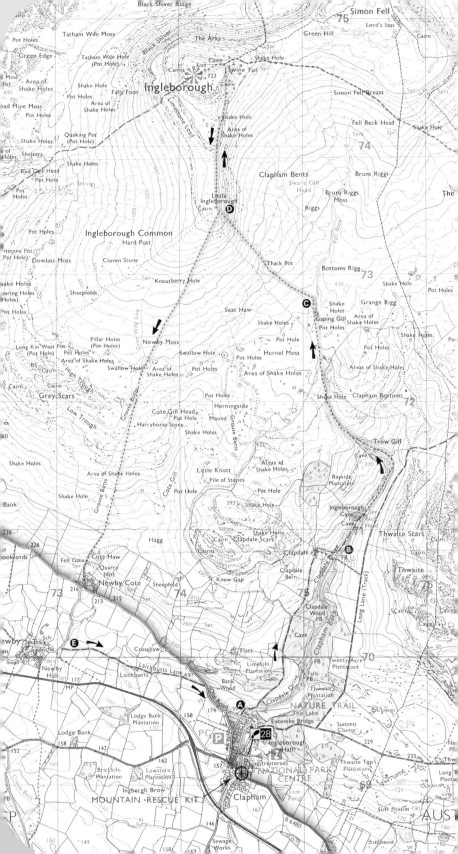

28 Ingleborough

Start:	Clapham
Distance:	8 miles (12·75 km)
Approximate time:	5 hours
Parking:	Clapham
Refreshments:	Pub and cafés at Clapham
Ordnance Survey maps:	Landranger 98 (Wensleydale & Upper Wharfedale), Outdoor Leisure 2 (Yorkshire Dales – Western area)

General description *The instantly recognisable bulk of Ingleborough (2,372 ft (723 m)), one of the 'Three Peaks', broods over the surrounding area and creates an almost irresistible magnet for keen hill walkers. Its lower slopes are full of interest: the attractive village of Clapham, the gentle scenery of Clapdale, the awesome chasm of Trow Gill and the dramatic entrance to Gaping Gill, while the higher slopes, though somewhat featureless in themselves, inevitably provide extensive and splendid views. Although the ascent is lengthy, it is not particularly strenuous, apart from the final haul to the summit, and involves no particular difficulties but, because of the lack of landmarks and the stretches of the route where there is no visible path, this walk should not be attempted in poor weather or misty conditions except by experienced hill walkers able to use a compass.*

Turn right out of the car park, almost immediately left over a foot-bridge and right again to follow the other side of Clapham Beck up to the top of the village. Here turn left and, after about 100 yards (92 m) turn right, at a public footpath sign for Ingleborough, Gaping Gill and Ingleborough Cave, along a walled track (**A**). The track gives good views over the woodlands of the Ingleborough Hall estate on the right and, beyond that, over open moorland. Climbing gently all the while, pass through two gates to emerge into more open country, shortly reaching a farm. Continue through the farmyard and, after passing through a gate at the far end, turn right at a sign for Ingleborough Cave.

Drop down steeply to join Clapham Beck and turn left (**B**) along a well surfaced track that follows the beck on the right through the attractive valley of Clapdale. Passing the entrance to Ingleborough Cave on the left (open to the public), continue over a footbridge and through a gate by a stile. Soon after the track bends to the left into a dry valley, go through a gate by a ladder stile to enter the almost perpendicular-sided, limestone gorge of Trow Gill. Proceed through the damp and gloomy chasm, climbing a rocky path at the far end where the gorge narrows to just a few feet. Emerging at the top, continue along a path by a wall on the left, eventually climbing some steps in that wall. Immediately ahead lies the distinctive bulk of Ingleborough.

Now follow a clear path across the bare, open, treeless moorland, soon passing the wire fence around the entrance to Gaping Gill (**C**). This is probably the most dramatic pot-hole in England. Fell Beck, one of many streams draining the slopes of Ingleborough, suddenly plunges through a large 'gape' or hole, down a 360 ft (110 m) shaft into a huge cavern the size of a cathedral. Keeping to the left of the Gill, continue along a path that bears left, away from the beck, and climbs steeply up to the cairn on Little Ingleborough (**D**), both a resting place and the launch pad for the final ¾ mile (1 km) to the top.

Continue ahead, climbing even more steeply up a rocky path that heads in a straight line towards the summit. Near the top the track flattens out and, from these windswept heights, there is a dramatic all-round view taking in Whernside and Pen-y-ghent (the other two 'Three Peaks'), Upper Ribblesdale and, to the west, the Forest of Bowland.

Retrace your steps as far as the cairn on Little Ingleborough (**D**) and, just a few yards past it, bear right off the original route, heading downhill across the rough, featureless moorland of Newby Moss. At this point there is no visible path and, because the surroundings are so bare, few landmarks, but keep in a straight line, following a shallow valley and descending quite steeply. When you see the village of Newby ahead, it will act as a good landmark and you continue in the direction of the village, eventually leaving the rough moorland and making for the corner of a wall. Keep ahead by the wall on the right to a ladder stile, climb over and carry on down a walled track, past a farm on the left, to a road.

The easiest way back to Clapham is to turn left along the road, but a more interesting alternative is to cross over and walk along the lane ahead, signposted Newby. Just before entering the village, turn sharp left at a public bridle-way sign (**E**), climb a stile a few yards ahead and follow a sunken green track, walled in places, called Laithbutts Lane, for about ¾ mile (1 km). Keep straight ahead past farm buildings where there is a break in the walled track, through two gates and continue ahead by a wall, and later a hedge, on the left. Go through another gate to rejoin the walled track and carry on up to the road. Turn right for the short distance back to Clapham village and car park.

Useful organisations

The Countryside Commission,
John Dower House, Crescent Place,
Cheltenham, Gloucestershire GL50 3RA.
Tel: 0242 21381

The National Trust,
36 Queen Anne's Gate, London SW1H
9AS. Tel: 01-222 9251
(Yorkshire Regional Office, 27 Tadcaster
Road, York YO2 2QG. Tel: 0204 702021)

Council for National Parks,
45 Shelton Street, London WC2H 9HS.
Tel: 01-240 3603

The Yorkshire Dales National Park,
Colvend, Hebden Road, Grassington,
Skipton, North Yorkshire BD23 5LB.
Tel: 0756 752748

National Park Authority Visitor Centres
can be found at:

Aysgarth Falls (Tel: 096 93424)

Clapham (Tel: 046 85419)

Grassington (Tel: 0756 752748)

Hawes (Tel: 096 97450)

Malham (Tel: 072 93363)

Sedbergh (Tel: 0587 20125)

Yorkshire and Humberside Tourist Board,
312 Tadcaster Road, York YO2 2HF.
Tel: 0904 707961

Yorkshire Dales Society,
152 Main Street, Addingham, via Ilkley,
West Yorkshire LS29 0LY.
Tel: 0943 607868

The Ramblers' Association,
1/5 Wandsworth Road, London
SW8 2LJ. Tel: 01-582 6878

The Forestry Commission,
Information Branch, 231 Costorphine
Road, Edinburgh EH12 7AT.
Tel: 031 334 0303

The Youth Hostels Association,
Trevelyan House, 8 St Stephen's Hill,
St Albans, Hertfordshire AL1 2DY.
Tel: 0727 55215

The Long Distance Walkers' Association,
Lodgefield Cottage, High Street,
Flimwell, Wadhurst, East Sussex
TN5 7PH. Tel: 058 087 341

The Council for the Protection of Rural
England,
4 Hobart Place, London SW1W 0HY.
Tel: 01-235 5959

Ordnance Survey
Romsey Road, Maybush, Southampton
SO9 4DH
Tel: 0703 792764/5 or 792749

Ordnance Survey maps of the Yorkshire Dales

The Yorkshire Dales is covered by Ordnance Survey 1:50 000 scale (1 ¼ inches to 1 mile) Landranger map sheets 98 and 99. These all-purpose maps are packed with information to help you explore the area. Viewpoints, picnic sites, places of interest, caravan and camping sites are shown, as well as public rights of way information such as footpaths and bridle-ways.

To examine the Yorkshire Dales in more detail and especially if you are planning walks, Ordnance Survey Outdoor Leisure maps at 1:25 000 (2 ½ inches to 1 mile) scale are ideal. Three such maps cover the area:

Sheet 2 — Yorkshire Dales
           (Western area)
Sheet 10 — Yorkshire Dales
           (Southern area)
Sheet 30 — Yorkshire Dales
           (Northern and Central area)

Areas not available in the Outdoor Leisure map series are instead covered by Pathfinder maps. Also at 1:25 000 (2 ½ inches to 1 mile), these are the perfect maps for walkers.

To look at the area surrounding the Yorkshire Dales, Ordnance Survey Routemaster maps at 1:250 000 (1 inch to 4 miles) scale will prove most useful. Sheet 5 (Northern England) and Sheet 6 (East Midlands and Yorkshire) are relevant.

Ordnance Survey maps and guides are available from most booksellers, stationers and newsagents.

Index